THE
CALL
TO
CONNECT
WITH
SPIRIT

EILEEN MARLOWE

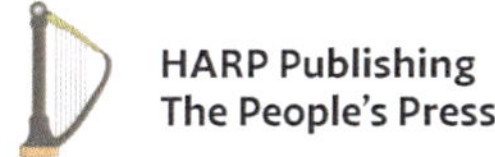

HARP Publishing
The People's Press

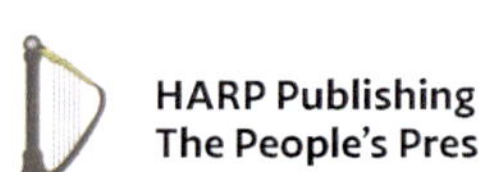

**HARP Publishing
The People's Press**

216 Clydesdale Road
Clydesdale, Nova Scotia
B2G 2K9 CANADA
tryhealingarts.ca

Information about purchasing copies of this book can be obtained from the publishers.

harppeoplespress@gmail.com

Graphic Design: Catharine Barker, National Graphics
Copy Editor: E. Lisa Moses

Catalogue-in-Publication data is on file with Library and Archives Canada

ISBN: 978-1-990137-50-1

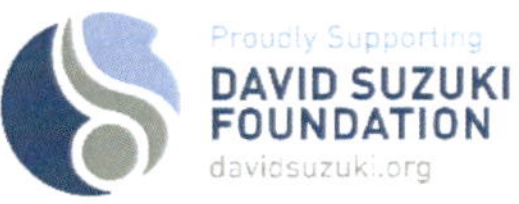
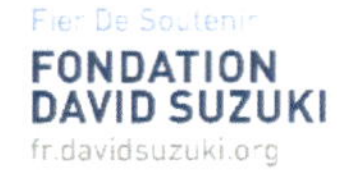
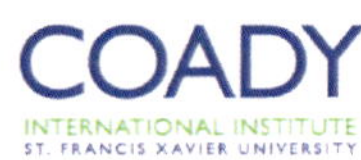

The Circle of Abundance Indigenous Program, Coady International Institute, St. Francis Xavier University: https://coady.stfx.ca/circle-of-abundance; and David Suzuki Foundation (one nature): https://davidsuzuki.org will receive 20% of all sales, distributed equally.

THIS
BOOK IS
ABOUT FORGING
CONNECTIONS WITH
SPIRIT AND LEVERAGING
THEM TO TRANSFORM YOUR LIFE

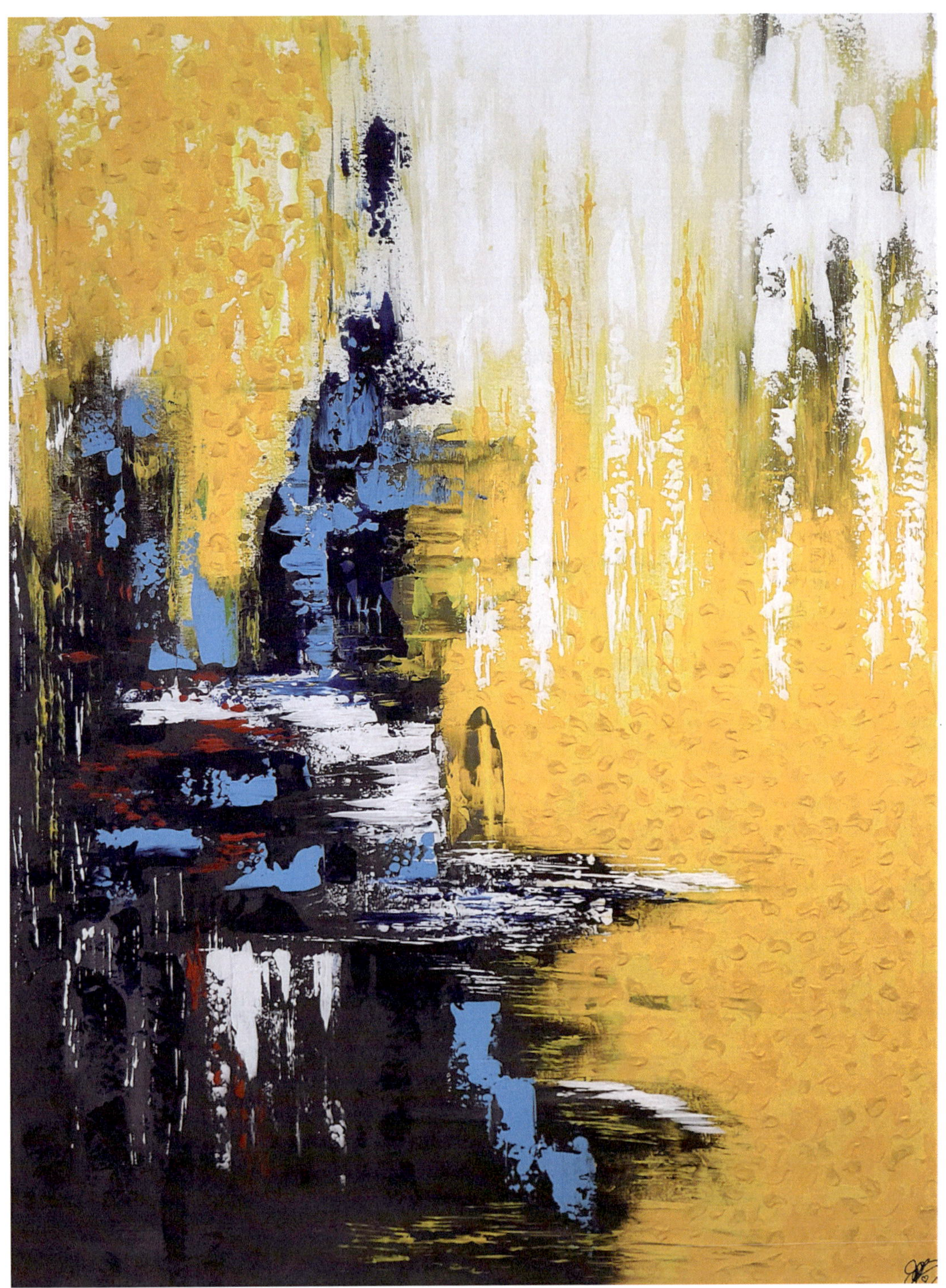

Strength

Acrylic on canvas, 2021
4 x 3 feet

This book is dedicated to Jiah and Connor.

Acknowledgments

I want to express my heartfelt gratitude and appreciation to several individuals who played a key role in my artistic expression. Whether they realized it or not, their influence encouraged me to paint and to write this book.

First and foremost, I would like to thank Will Gagnon, a climate change trailblazer and Kathryn Dykstra, an abstract artist. Both are non-Indigenous friends and amazing individuals who made it easy for me to write my first draft. Their willingness to listen as I presented my initial ideas and concepts made an immense difference in how I moved forward. I love you and thank you for coming into my life.

I am grateful to my children, Jiah and Connor, for their support and encouragement to paint. I am also pleased that my son witnessed firsthand the transformation in me as I learned to meditate and paint. I love you both so much. Use your medicine wisely and for the greater good.

I also want to express my gratitude to three men named "George," one of whom was my late father George Marlowe. All were instrumental in helping me embrace my spiritual identity.

Finally, I want to acknowledge those who provided invaluable feedback and suggested edits. You know who you are.

Marci cho (Thank you),

Eileen

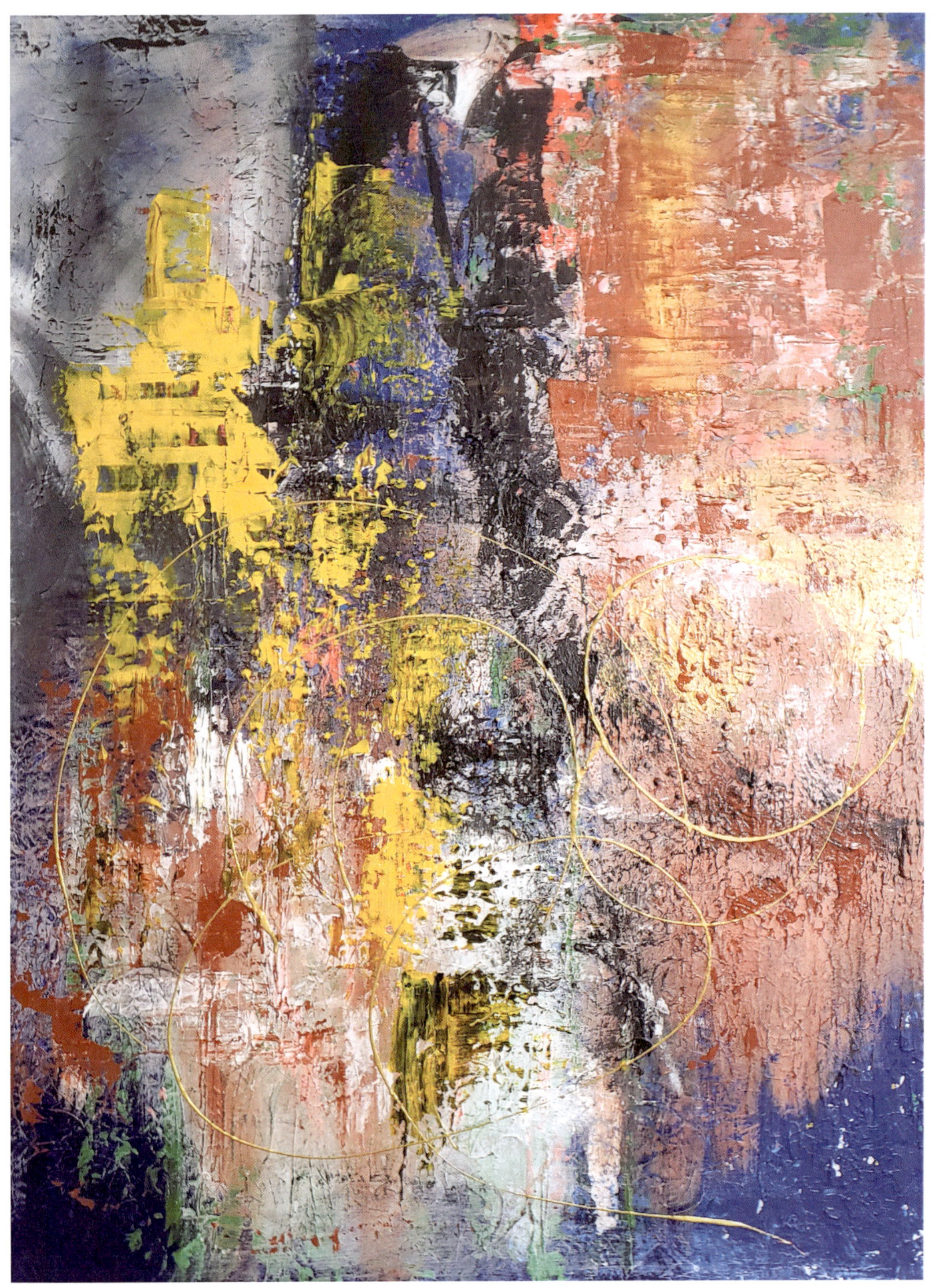

Queen

Acrylic on canvas, 2021
4 x 3 feet

INTRODUCTION

Becoming whole by acknowledging my spiritual identity

In 2020, I was plagued by persistent thoughts to meditate—a concept that was new to me. I finally realized that the urge was a sign from Spirit to begin identifying my spiritual identity.

Up to this point, my sense of self was based on Western ways of living and being: a "divide, conquer and compete" mentality that left me feeling inadequate. Throughout my life, I had been off centre because I was not recognizing an essential missing part—my spirituality.

In March 2020, I heeded those thoughts and embarked on a life-changing process. This meant acknowledging my spiritual identity, learning the language of my spiritual guides, and establishing two-way communications with them.

I had no idea that I was on the cusp of profound change, nor did I know that I would discover the gift of self-empowerment within me. It's a gift that captured my attention and one to which we all have access. That gift, my

beautiful reader, sits right inside our hearts and is the doorway to dialoguing with our spiritual guides.

The transformation was so deep and life-changing that I am eager to share my findings with others who may be longing for clarity about their spirituality.

Through this enlightening experience, I explain the role of my spiritual guides, my interaction with them and the resulting transformations. I discuss:

1) How they got my attention through insightful **thoughts** and guided me to peaceful spaces that empowered me in ways I never thought possible.

2) How they communicated with me through the symbology of dreams and abstract art, some of which you will see in this book.

3) How I established and now maintain a relationship with them by releasing the past, creating self-awareness and committing to daily meditation.

A voyage of discovery

Initially, I discovered that perceptive **thoughts** came from my heart. Later, I realized that my heart was the conduit for Spirit to communicate with me. And I am now making a conscious effort toward being the architect and director of my own life.

I had been living a life based on ego, reactions and forced proactivity, even if those conflicted with messages from my heart. Through my acknowledgment of heart (Spirit), I embraced true love and joy, which have led to a renewed sense of vigour and wholeness.

By listening to Spirit guidance, I have made significant changes in my life. These include meditating daily, becoming an abstract artist and now, evolving into a writer of books. I have embraced my fears and insecurities and use them to empower myself. I am newly aware of how my body responds to people and the environment, and identifies those I should avoid—and most importantly, distrust.

And the journey is one I am happy to share.

> Note that I bold the word **thought(s)** to indicate communications from heart space/Spirit and italicize ***thinking*** as thoughts from headspace/brain/ego.

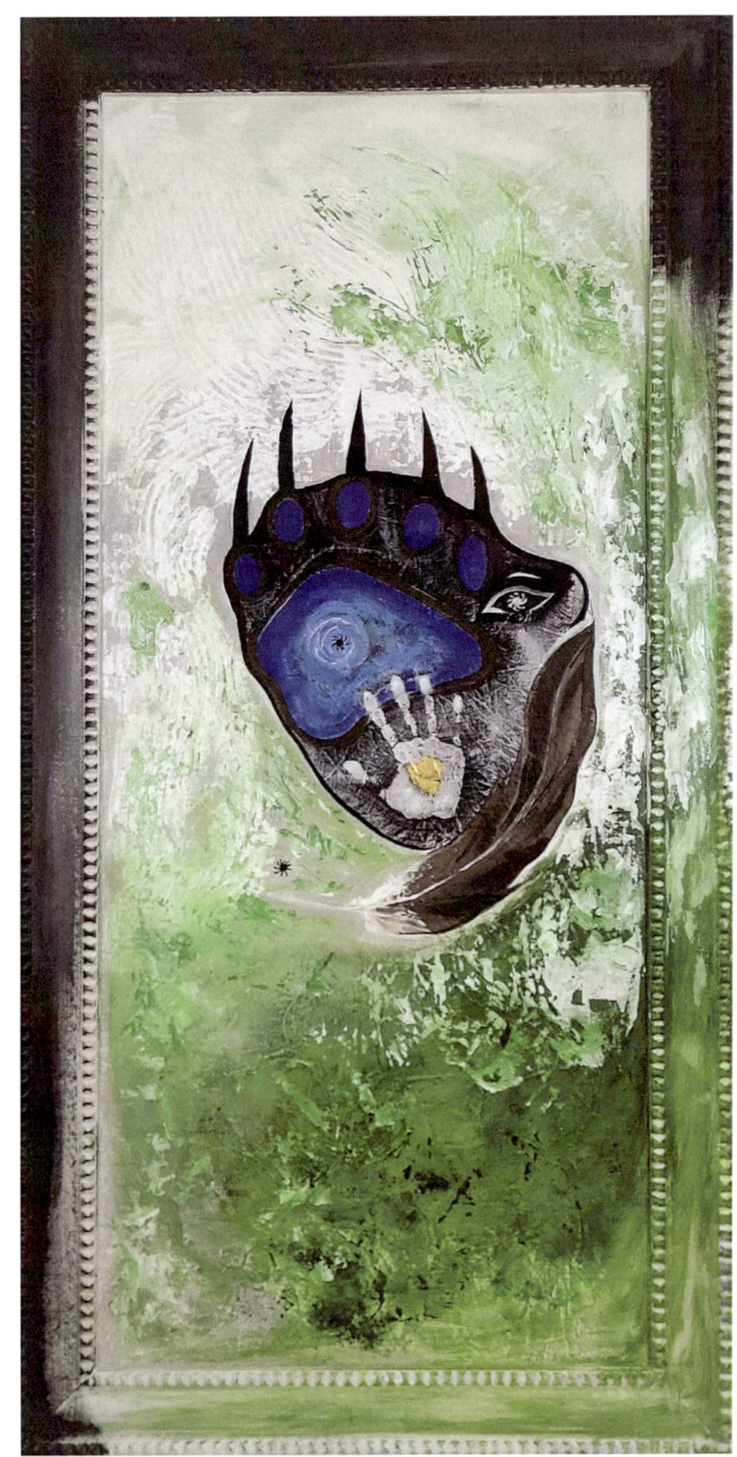

I AM THE MEDICINE THAT
SITS WITHIN YOU.

Spirit guides

Acrylic on board, 2023
5 x 2 feet

DREAMS

First encounters with Spirit guides

Over the course of my life, I have had four distinct and significant dreams to which I felt very connected. Each featured an extraterrestrial being (Spirit) that took the form of familiar wildlife.

Dream One:
Meeting the Grizzly Bear Spirit

It was autumn, and I was alone in an empty cabin in the woods. I stood in the centre facing the open door through which I could see fallen leaves blanketing the earth.

The cabin had two windows, one on each side. Through the left window I saw a huge grizzly bear sauntering toward me. (I sensed the bear was female.) I felt calm and confident, and expected her to come through the door. However, she walked past the doorway and around the cabin to the right-hand window. There, she stood on her hind legs and leaned on the window ledge, looking at me through the mesh screen.

Then, telepathically or through **thoughts**, the bear told me to walk over and stand in front of her. Unafraid, I did that and looked directly into her face.

I recall feeling astounded to be standing so close to her and gazing into her beautiful chocolate eyes. They stared at me with sheer love, grace and strength—and exuded immense power.

I felt captivated by her tenderness toward me, as I had never felt such love from anyone in my life before. At that moment I got to know true love and what it feels like, and I am so grateful for that.

After we had locked eyes for some time, she placed her paw on the window screen and telepathically told me to touch it with my hand. We continued to stare at each other in silence while her loving eyes and gentle presence penetrated me to the core.

After some time, she transmitted the message, "Okay, I must go now." She then turned and headed back into the woods.

My interpretation:

This dream introduced me to the notion of telepathy or imprinted **thoughts**. The bear let me know that I would be alone for a period in my life during which time I must learn to love myself. She offered me the gifts of enormous love, strength and protection— and communicated that I would have the fortitude to overcome anything. Lastly, she advised that I would need to have faith and trust, and that she would always be there for me.

Dream Two:
Meeting the Bison Spirit

It was summertime, and I was walking alone on the shoulder of a highway. Up ahead, I saw a huge bison standing on the road. He stared at me, but I felt no fear and gazed at him calmly while walking past. I then climbed back onto the roadway.

My interpretation:

I felt the bison was relaying the message that I would have to walk alone to learn. He imprinted on me that once I extracted my internal power to heal myself, I would be able to climb back onto the road of love and compassion. When I embraced my internal strength and grace, I would walk the path that was intended for me—one where I can truly be of help to others.

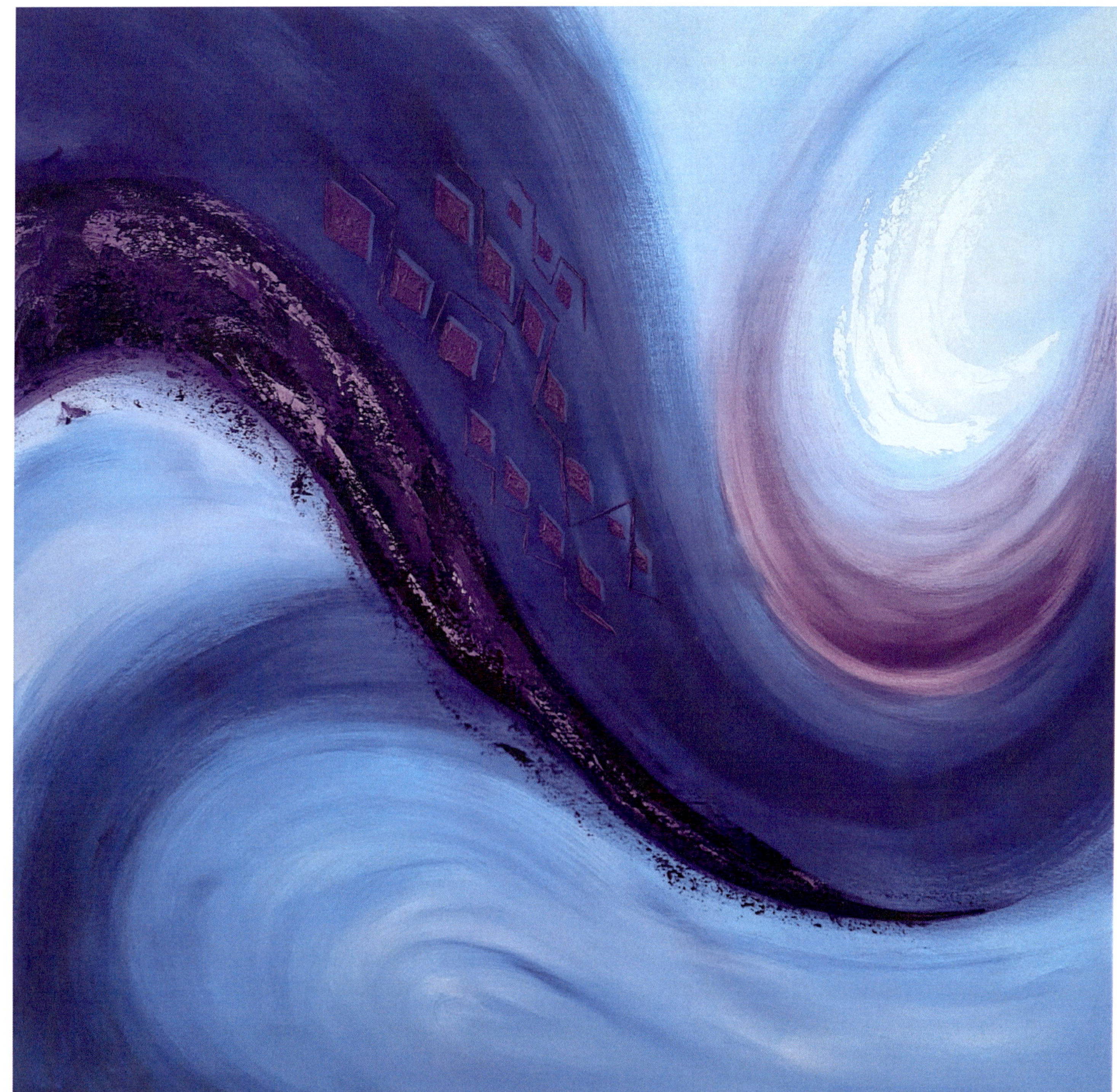

Scorpio

Acrylic on canvas, 2022
4 x 4 feet

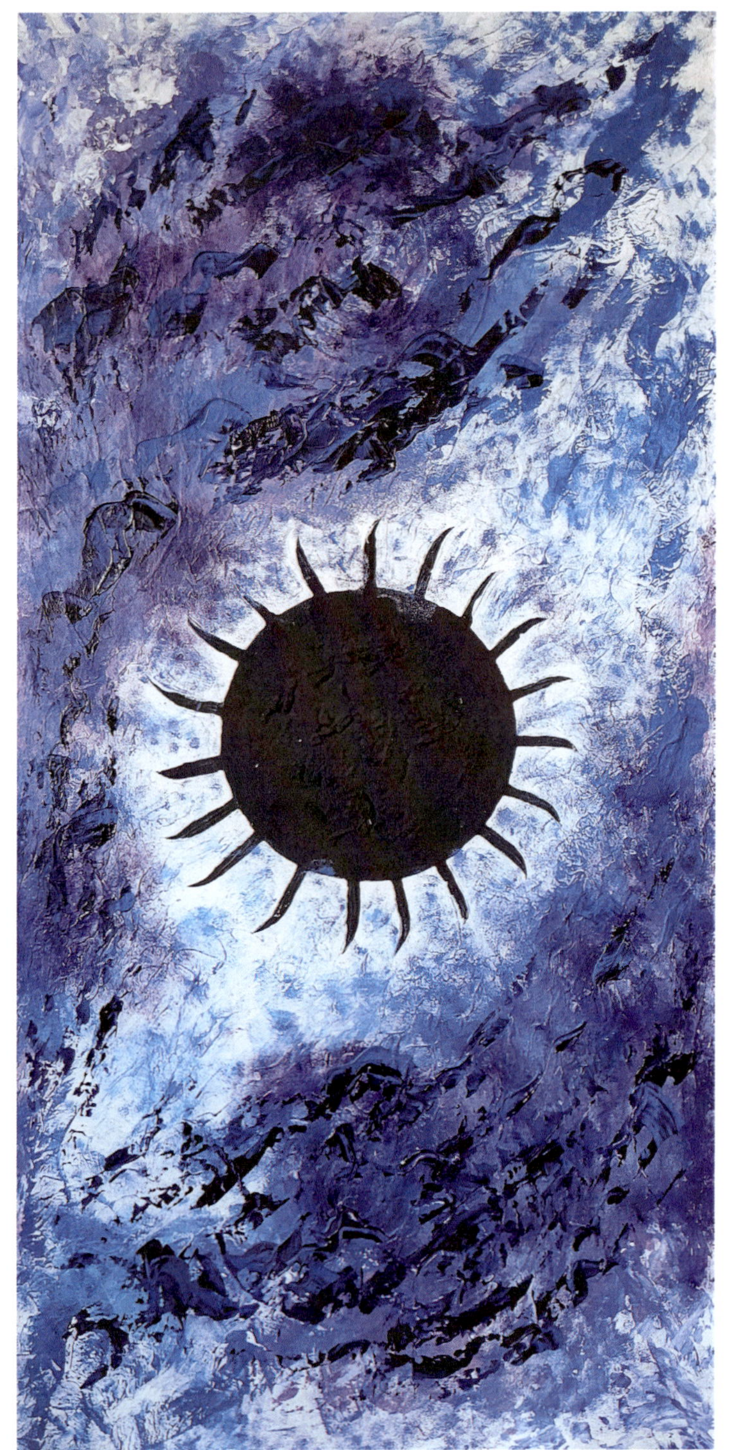

I AM EMBRACING THE MEDICINE WITHIN ME.

*Black Bug
medicine power*

Acrylic on board, 2021
4 x 2 feet

Dream Three:
Meeting the Black Bug Spirit

This dream featured a black bug and three sheets of blank white paper. I did not want to touch the bug with my bare hands, so I picked up one sheet and slid it under the insect. I folded the paper with the bug sitting in the middle and gently pressed it without squishing him. I then felt an incredibly powerful feeling that penetrated my arm and moved its way up into my shoulders. And I flung the bug and paper into the air.

My interpretation:

When I picked up the black bug even without touching him, he let me know how powerful he was by infusing my arm and shoulder with what felt like an electric current. The pieces of paper symbolized three views to consider for empowerment: high-ranking medicine power, personal medicine power and energy.

Spiritual energy

Acrylic on canvas, 2021
4 x 2 ½ feet

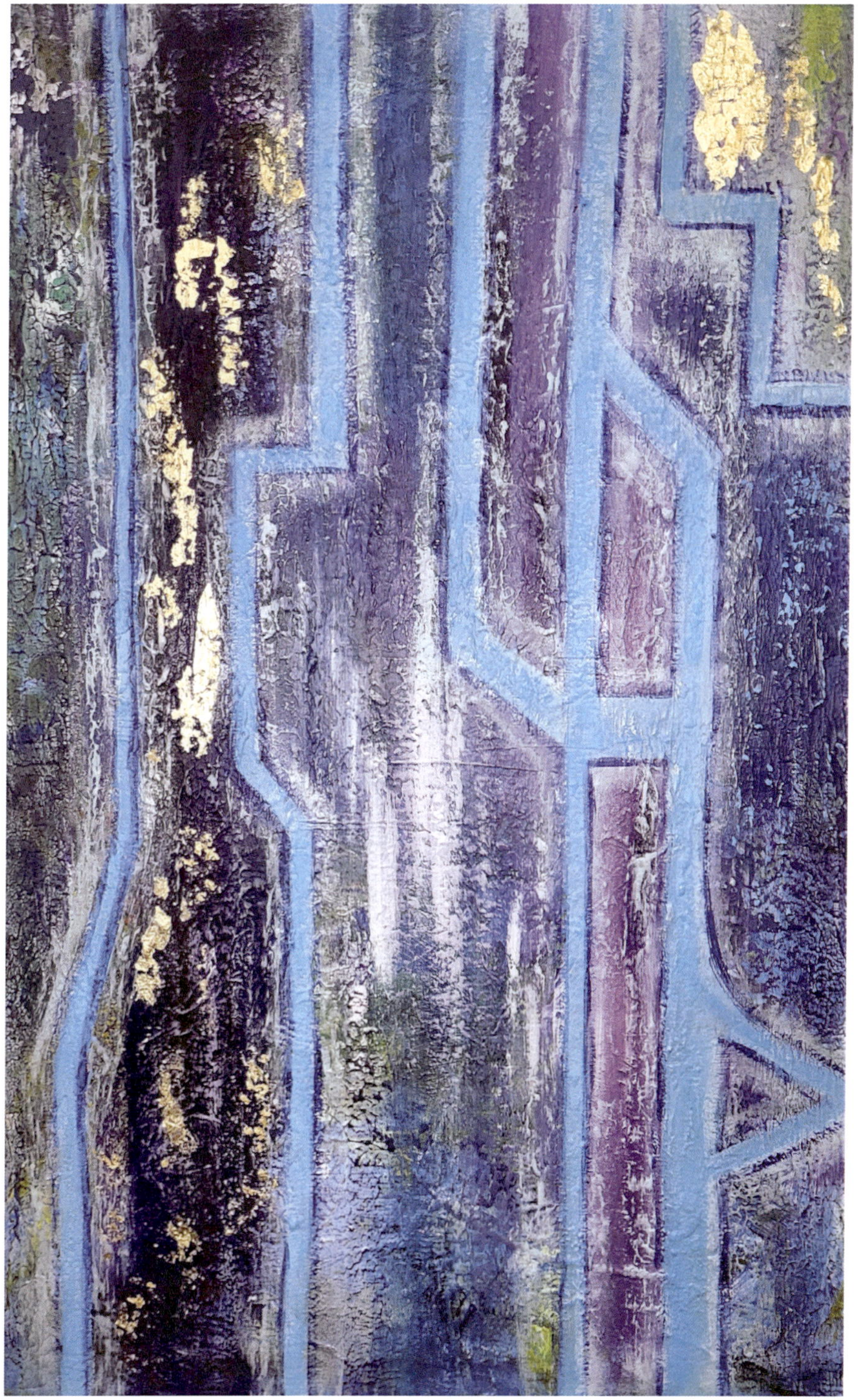

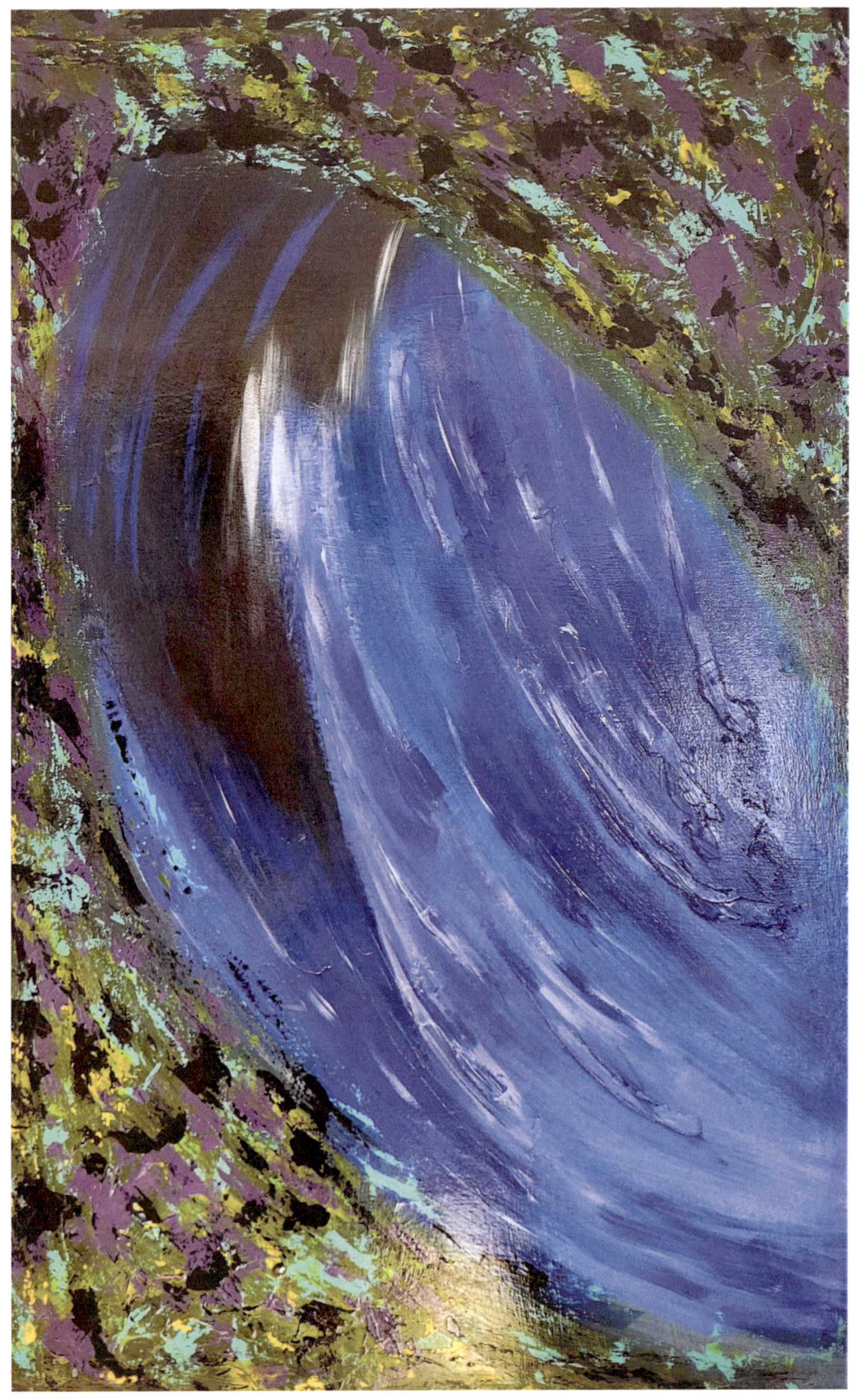

Dream Four:
Meeting the Eagle Spirit

In this dream, a huge eagle landed on my left
arm. I felt flabbergasted and utterly amazed
that my slender arm could handle the weight
of this big bird. In my astonishment, I was
trying to understand what was happening
while the eagle stared at me intently. He then
gently pecked my arm to snap me out of my
daze. I felt he wanted me to grab one of his
feathers, so with my right hand I clutched a
feather from his wing.

Majestic

Acrylic on canvas, 2021
4 x 2 ¹/₂ feet

My interpretation:

The eagle placed a heavy weight on me when he landed on my left arm. However, he knew that, with his guidance, I would be able to tolerate it.

He presented me with the gifts of sight and strategy. By offering me a wing feather, he let me know that I can soar to great heights and glide with grace back to earth. He also helped me see the imbalance that exists not only in my life, but also within our communities through the social structures we create and maintain.

With his strength and love, the eagle would help me glide gracefully and see the best path forward with the tiniest details. He let me know that it would be difficult, but I would be able to lift people with inspiration.

I AM STRATEGIC.

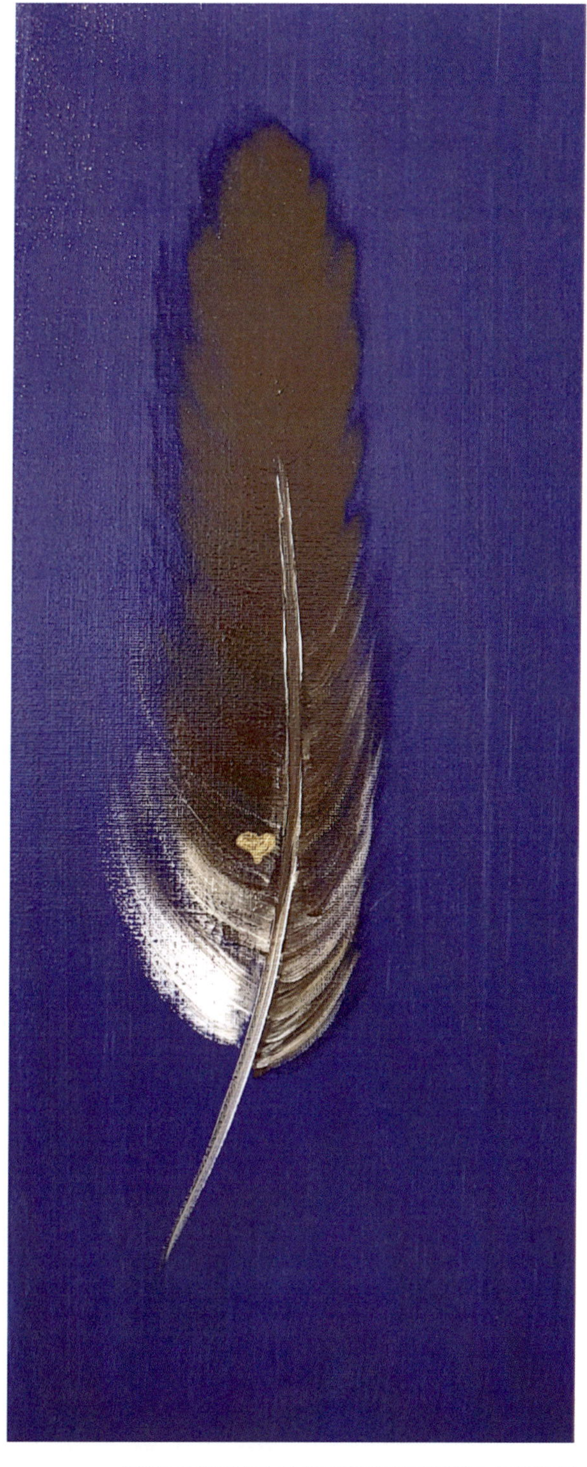

Eagle medicine power

Acrylic on canvas, 2023
8 x 20 inches

Messages from medicine

Our personal spiritual guides are like medicine. They manifest as the missing pieces in our day-to-day lives that exist to influence us and illustrate what is in our best interests. We need them to create balance not only within ourselves but also within our communities.

I grew up with stories of medicine power that intrigued me. But whenever I inquired, I was told that the power could be granted only by Spirit.

From my personal experience and spiritual guides, I am sharing two concepts of traditional medicine power and my contemporary perspective on the subject. And the black bug is a key character.

I AM YOUR MEDICINE.

Medicine power

Acrylic on canvas, 2023
2 x 2 feet

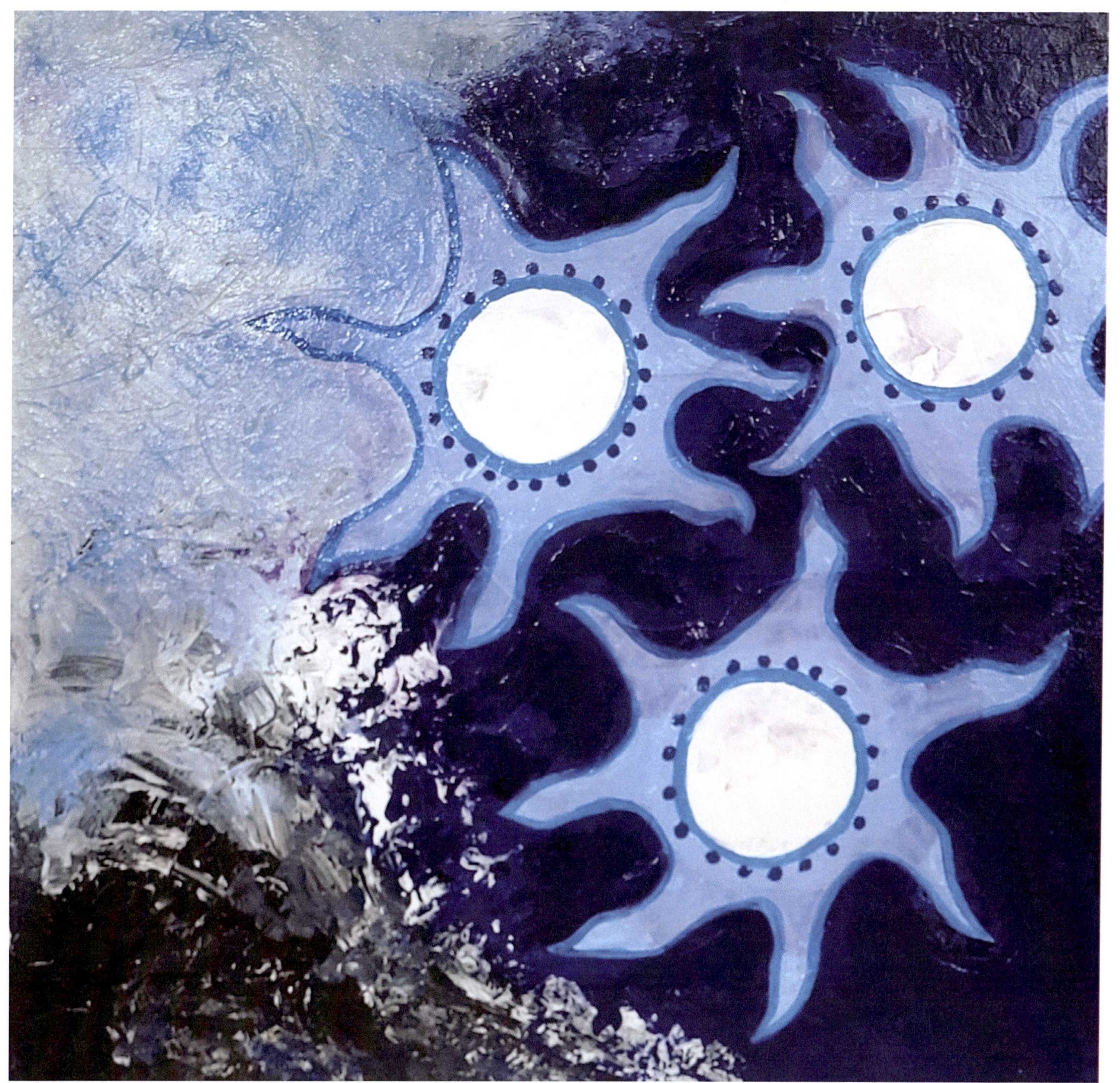

Message One:
True (high-ranking) medicine power

The first message from the black bug was that true (high-ranking) medicine power cannot be learned from books or any kind of written material. Flinging the black bug and white paper into the air is a symbol of that.

My understanding of medicine power was associated with medicine men and women who played an integral role in their tribes. They had the ability to heal people; some could even retrieve lost souls from deep within the earth and cosmos. Many could locate and track animals such as caribou for sustenance, as well as influence the weather.

Today, few medicine people exist. Those who claim the positions don't have the ability to heal others. If they could, our world would be filled with healthy people and communities.

Medicine men and women often abused their powers to hurt or kill their competitors and seize their advantages. While conflicts such as these divided tribes, healers were nevertheless revered in Indigenous cultures.

Leadership notes

Upon reflection, I've concluded that true medicine power is associated with leadership. True leaders have pure and compassionate hearts. They assume influential positions for not only themselves but also the collective. And they help create healthy communities.

Some of today's leaders, whether Indigenous or non-Indigenous, have created and sustained a culture of oppression. This divides our communities and casts our world into chaos. The fight for land and resources is prominent.

Most leaders, whether at the local, national or global level, do not want to work together in a meaningful way or share resources with fairness. Greed and hate propel them into divisions and wars. Their leadership styles and misuse of power hurt and kill people daily.

Add to this dire situation the drastic changes in our environment. As extreme consumers, we contribute to Mother Earth's angry tears through extreme floods, fires and earthquakes worldwide. We have lost our way.

A remedial step would be to select quality leaders who appreciate the importance of collaboration for the collective.

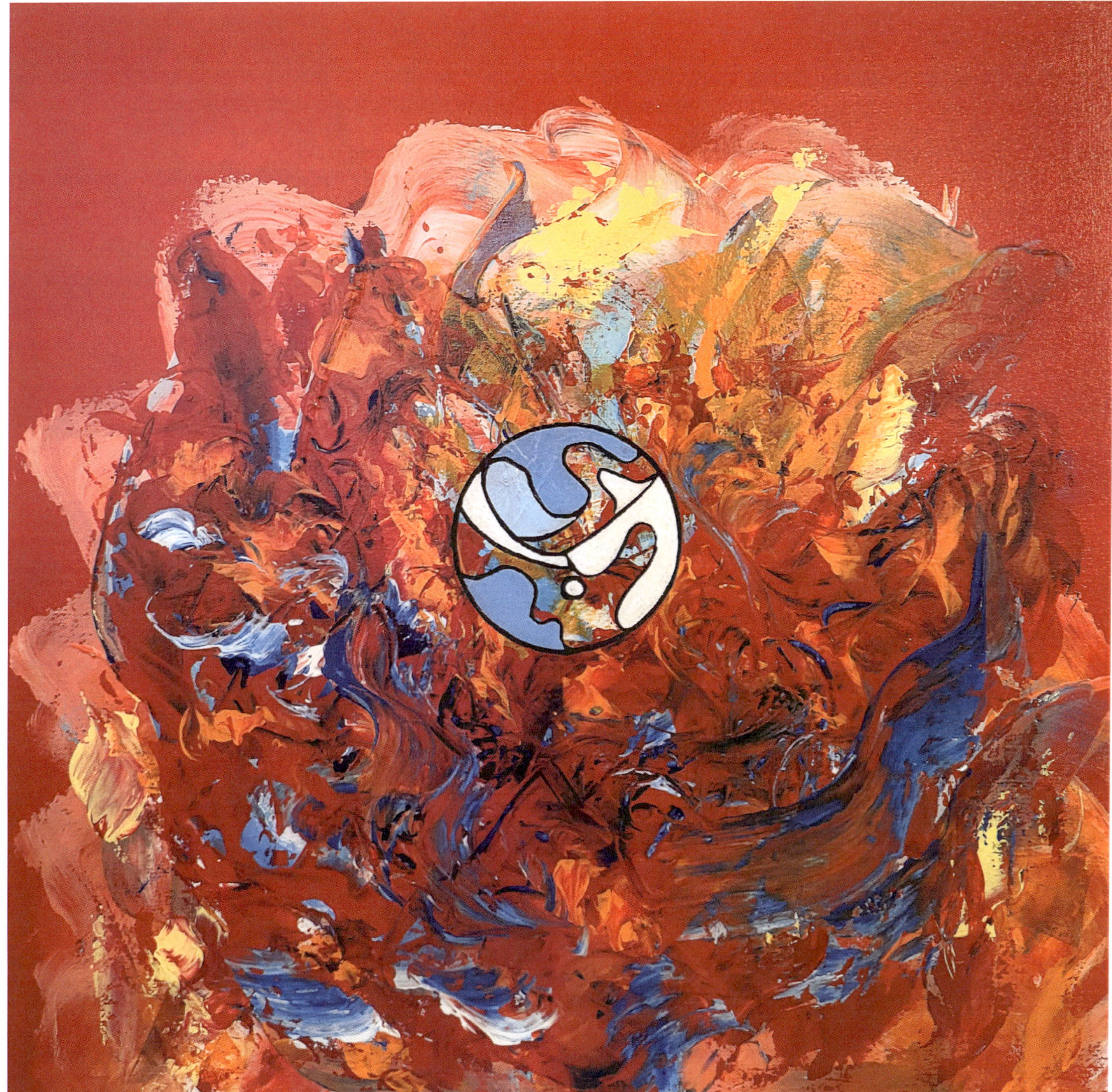

True leader

Acrylic on canvas, 2023
2 x 2 feet

Message Two:
Personal medicine power

The second message from the black bug was
to let me know that as individuals, we have
unknowingly given our personal medicine
powers away. This is also illustrated by flinging
the paper and black bug into the air.

We give our power away when we think solely
from our headspace (brain). I now recognize
that my feelings of disconnection or lack of
balance resulted from ignoring **thoughts**
from my heart space for wholesome living
and decision-making.

Message Three:
Energy

The third message from the black bug was to
introduce me to the notion of energy we hold
within our bodies and in the environment. To
adequately hold and confidently grasp the gift
of the black bug, we must clear the negative
energy inside our bodies through healthy
expression. That work includes meditating,
nurturing creativity, eating healthily and
maintaining nourishing relationships.

Our environment needs detoxification as
well. We must move toward clean energy
solutions that do not contribute to making
the planet sick.

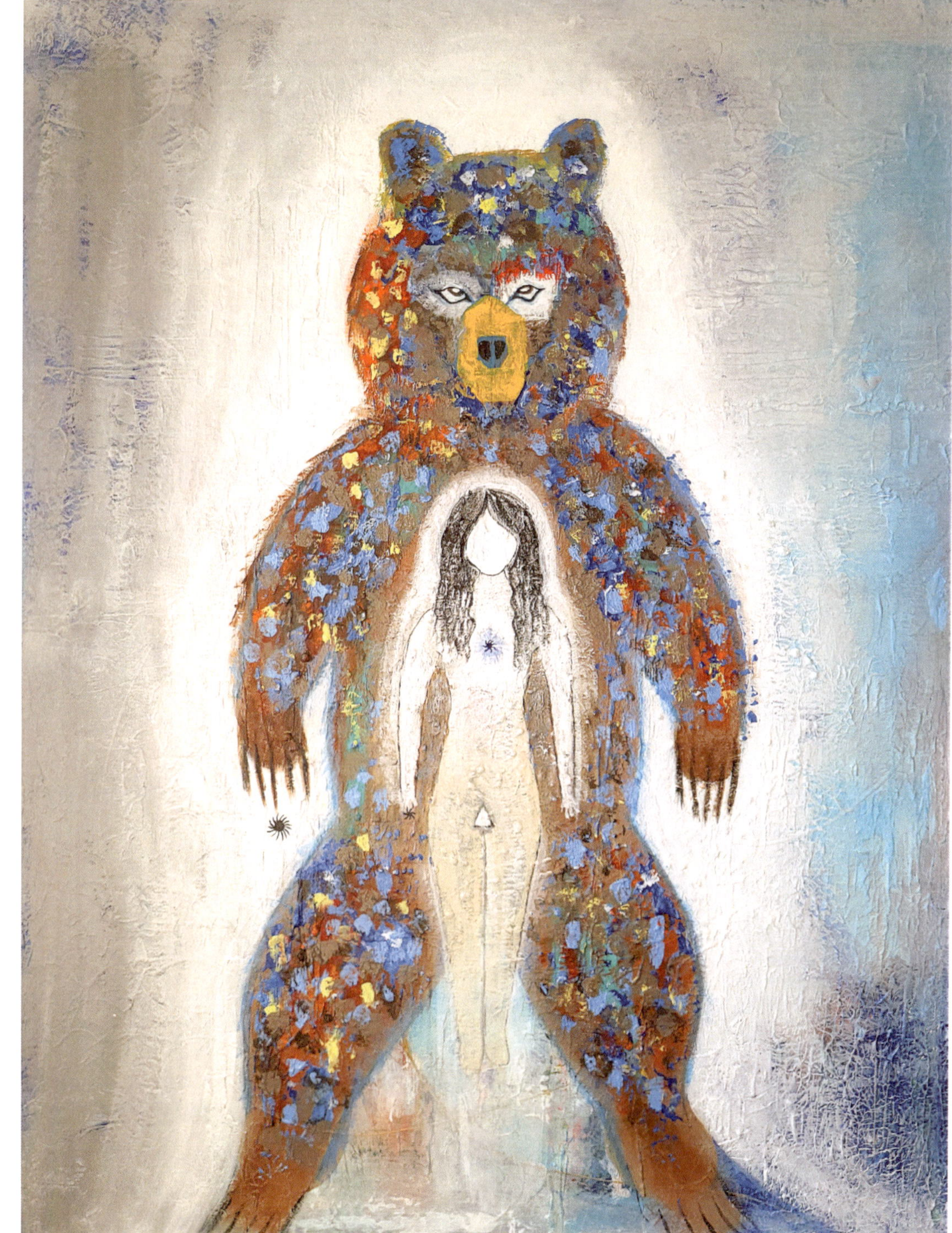

Grizzly Bear Spirit

Acrylic on canvas, 2022
4 x 3 feet

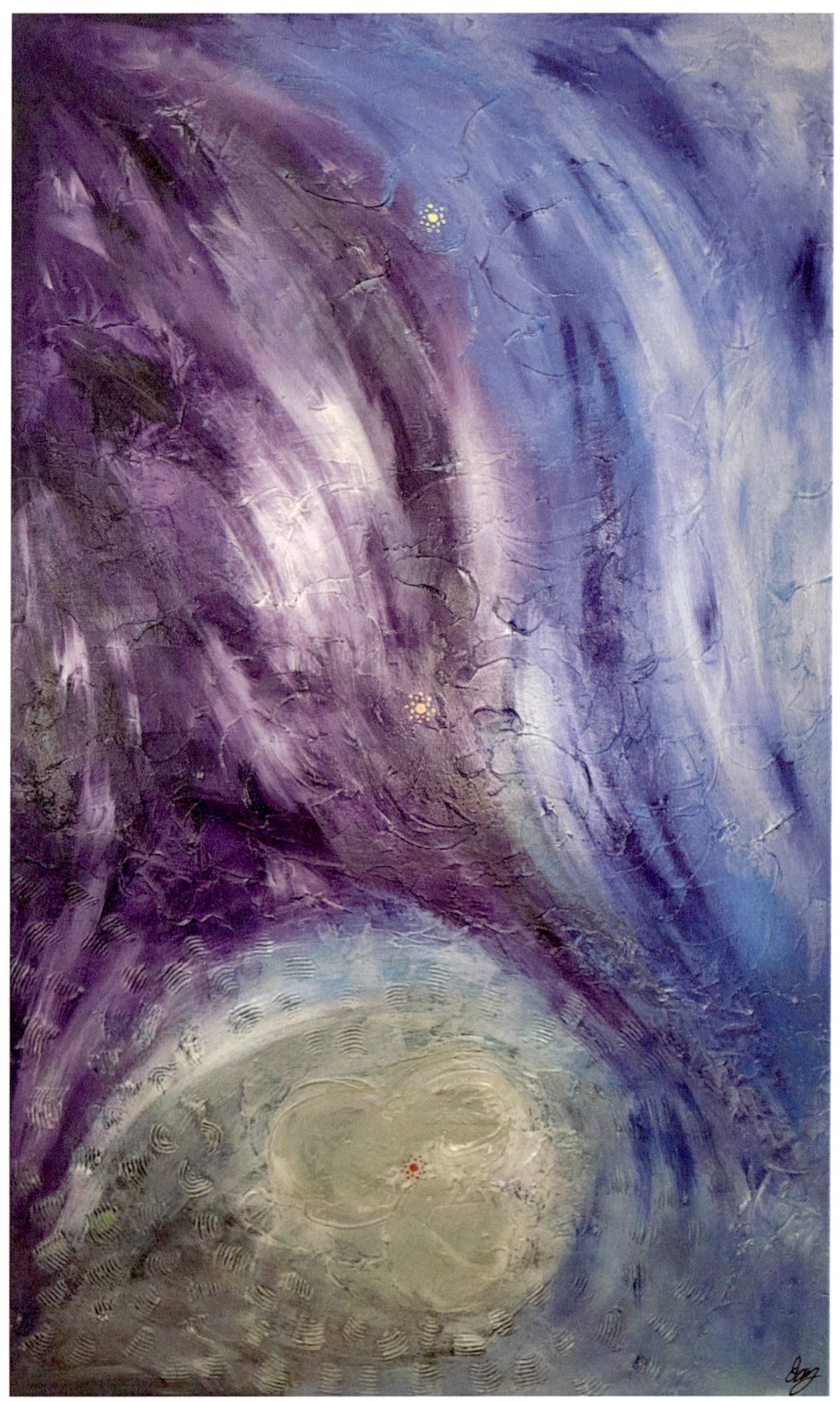

Bird family

Acrylic on canvas, 2020
5 x 3 feet

RECOGNIZING THE LANGUAGE OF SPIRIT

Spirit communicates through symbology and thoughts. Our task is to listen carefully and interpret its messages correctly.

Symbology

Symbology is a form of visual language. Through my dreams and abstract art, Spirit communicates the concepts of strategic guidance, healing and empowerment.

The symbols in my dreams provided me with opportunities to reflect on life's meaning when I awoke. By doing so, they were preparing me for what was to come.

Symbolism in my abstract art stirred emotions, created mental shifts and conveyed creative ideas for a more strategic approach to my life. As I painted, the colours, shapes and textures allowed me to go deeper and to gain clarity on strategic paths forward. Creative expression through abstract art has healed aspects of me that needed healing. And the beauty of this is that it was done in silence.

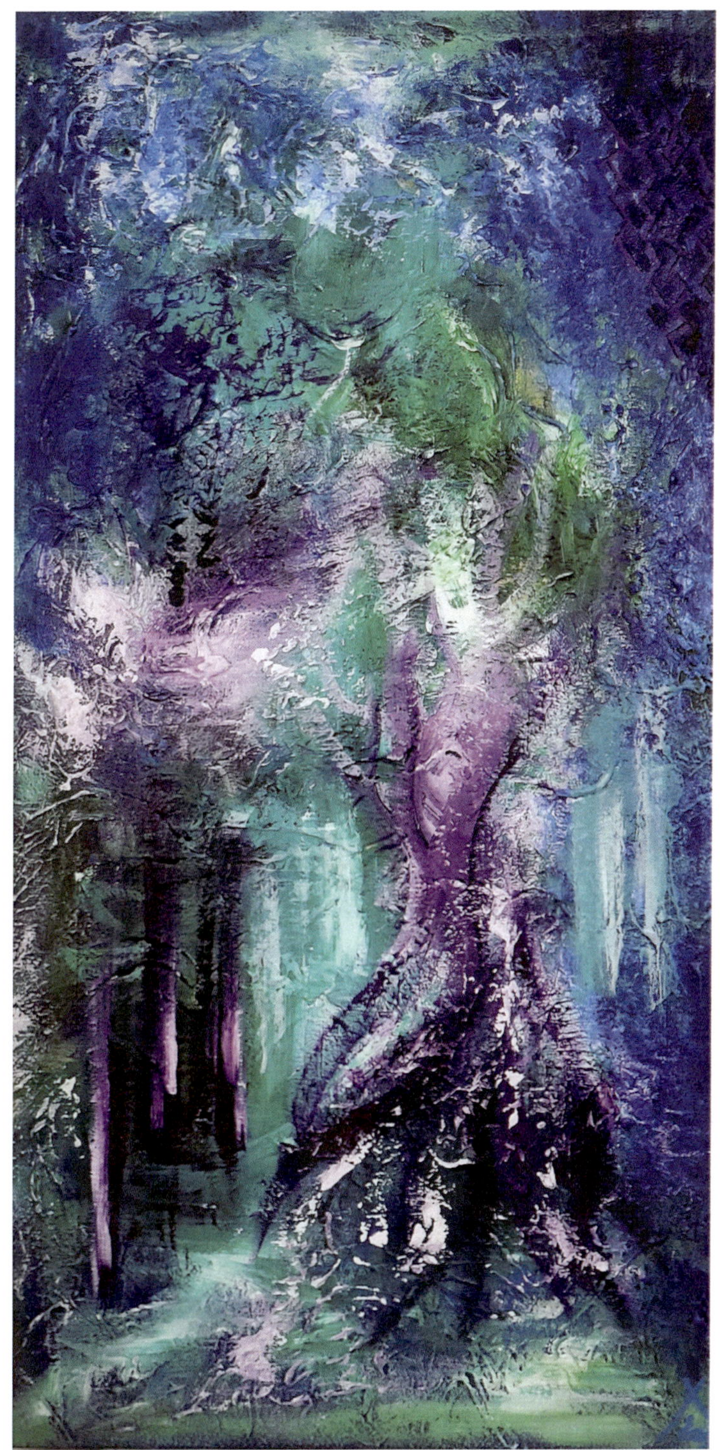

I am divine

Acrylic on canvas, 2022
4 x 2 feet

Thoughts

Many of us were not taught to think from our heart space, yet it is through our hearts that Spirit communicates with us.

I now recognize that throughout my life Spirit had always been communicating with me. However, through my own ignorance, I was unable to recognize the communication channels.

The path to distinguishing between thoughts from my headspace/brain/ego and **thoughts** from heart space was through self-awareness. I had to pay attention to myself throughout the day. In doing so, I was able to understand the characteristics and feelings associated with the types of thoughts I had.

Much of what I learned through our education system was solely brain-based (divide, conquer, compete, control). This often leads to dysfunction and unhealthy consumption, expressions and societal norms.

Trust was essential in establishing a relationship with my spiritual guides as I made life decisions based on communications from them. I therefore made a point of asking myself whether certain thoughts were coming from my headspace/brain/ego or heart space/Spirit.

Headspace/brain/ego thoughts

I realized that thoughts about what I desired in life were often based on established scenarios or fears. My ego was also involved in rationalizing or justifying wishes and actions. Thoughts from the brain could stem from dividing, conquering, competing and controlling mentalities.

I also noticed that some headspace/brain/ego **thinking** brought muscle tension.

Finally, I found thoughts from the brain can sometimes be ill-intentioned and misleading—and sometimes do not consider the highest good for me or others. An example would be remaining in an unhealthy dynamic with someone even though it did not feel right.

Heart space thoughts

In my quest to understand **thoughts** coming from my heart, I found them to be in stark contrast to brain thoughts because they come directly from Spirit. They do not involve scenario-building; rather, they feel like impressions or reminders.

Heart-based thoughts can be surprising: they are soft, subtle and seemingly from nowhere, but at times can be very clear, persistent and direct.

Thoughts from heart space are not ill-intentioned or misleading, and consider the highest good for me and others.

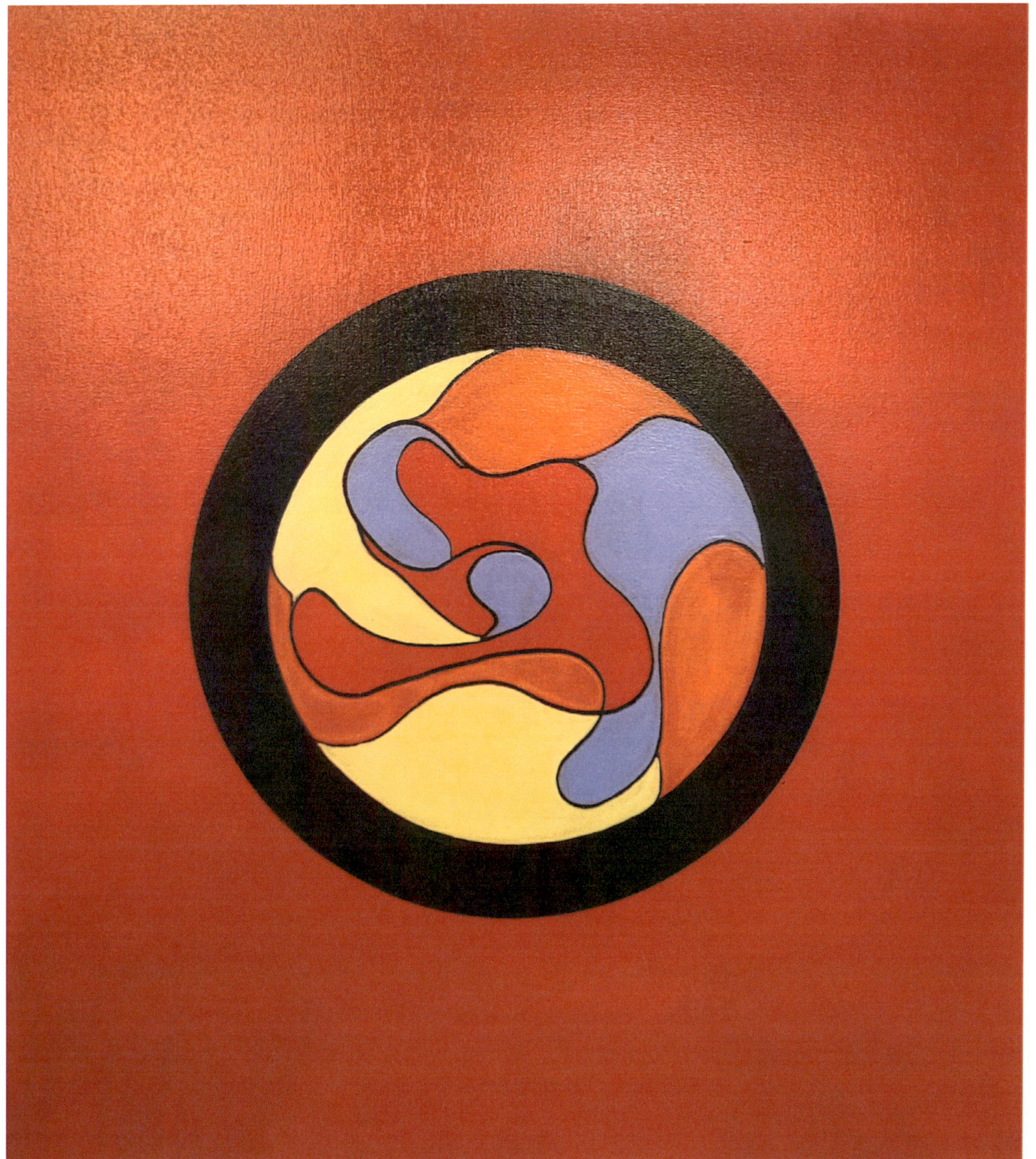

Breakthrough

Acrylic on canvas, 2022
2 x 2 feet

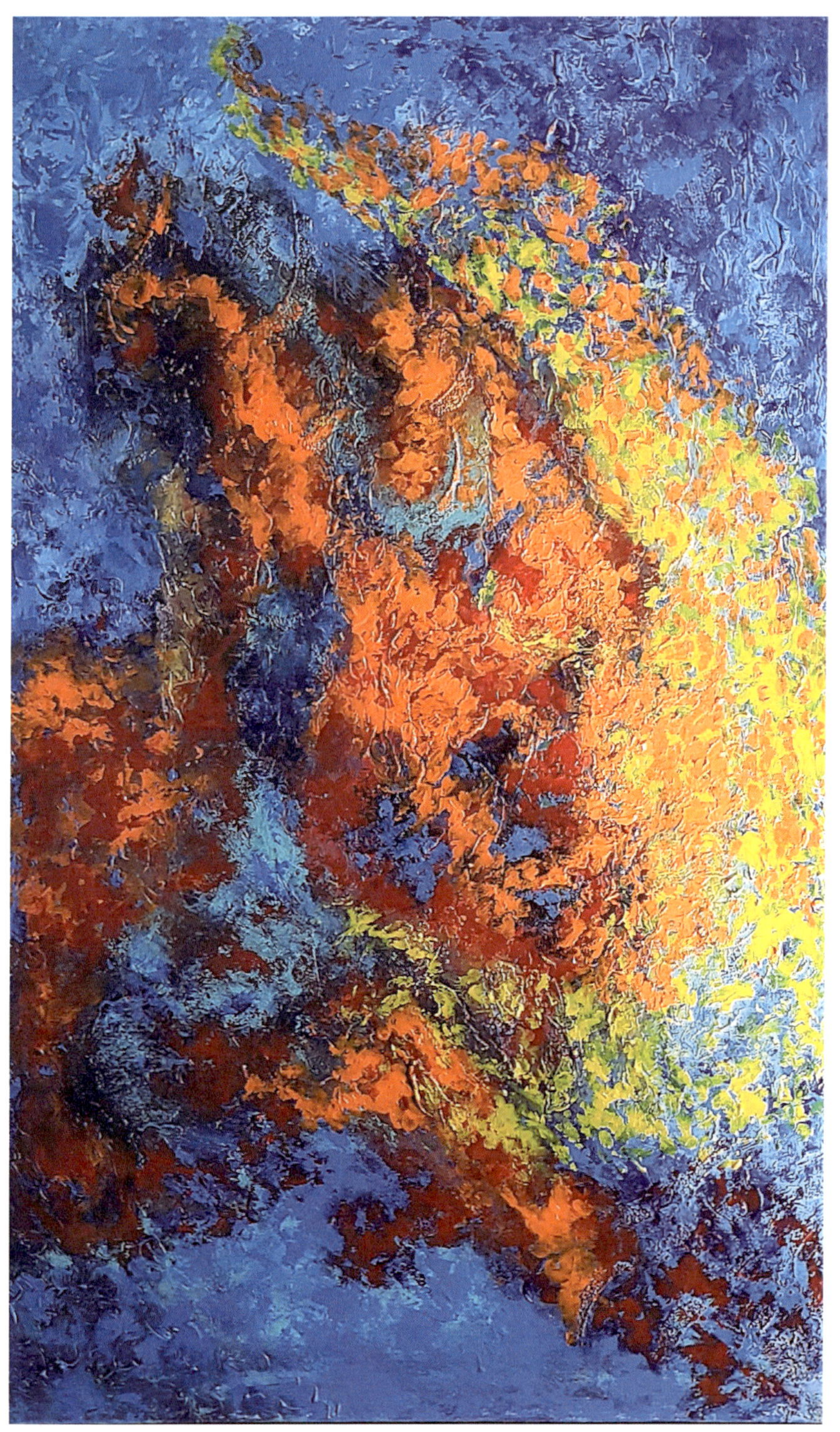

Heart focus

Acrylic on canvas, 2020
3 x 2 feet

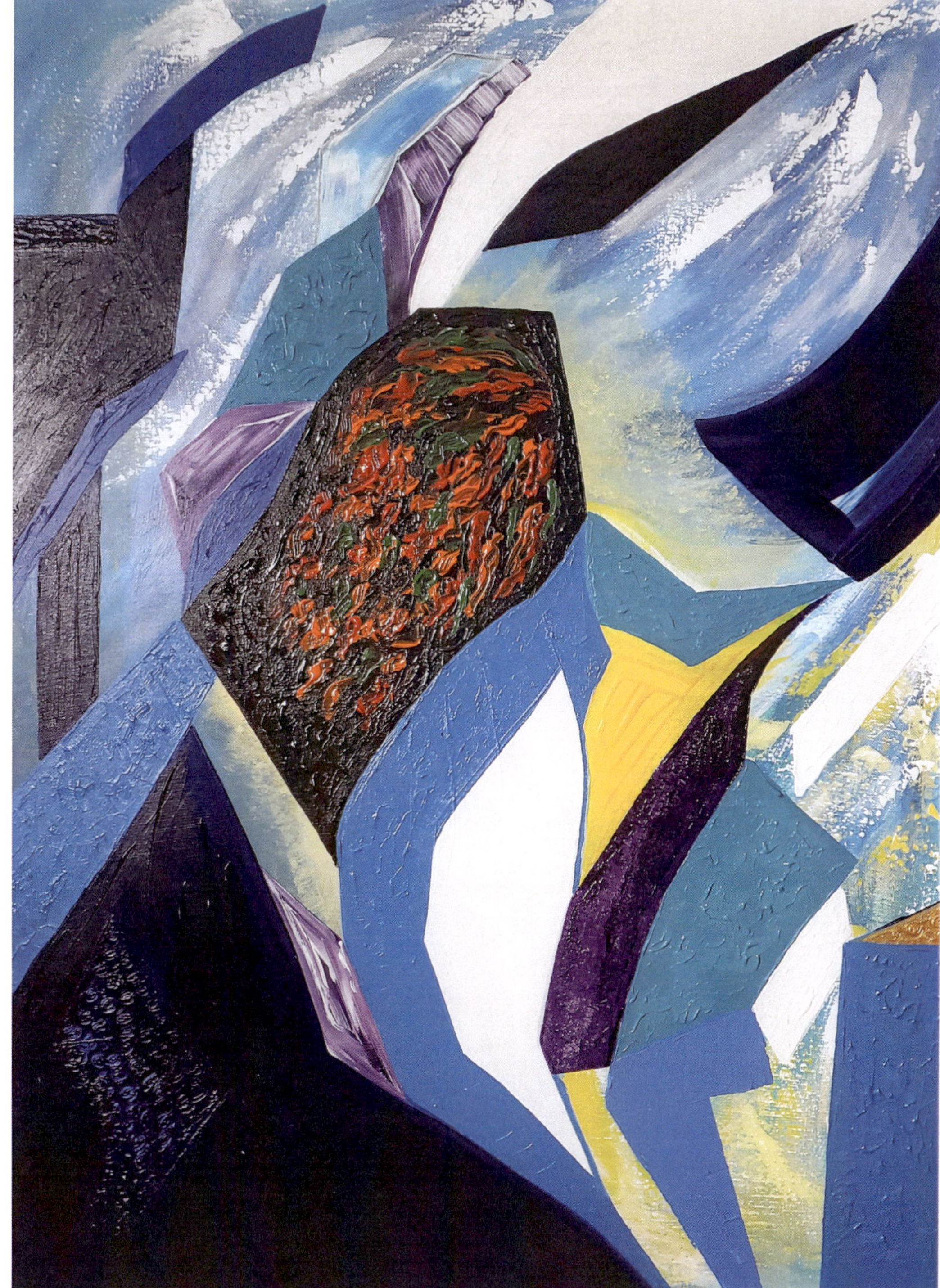

Perspective matters

Acrylic on canvas, 2021
4 x 3 feet

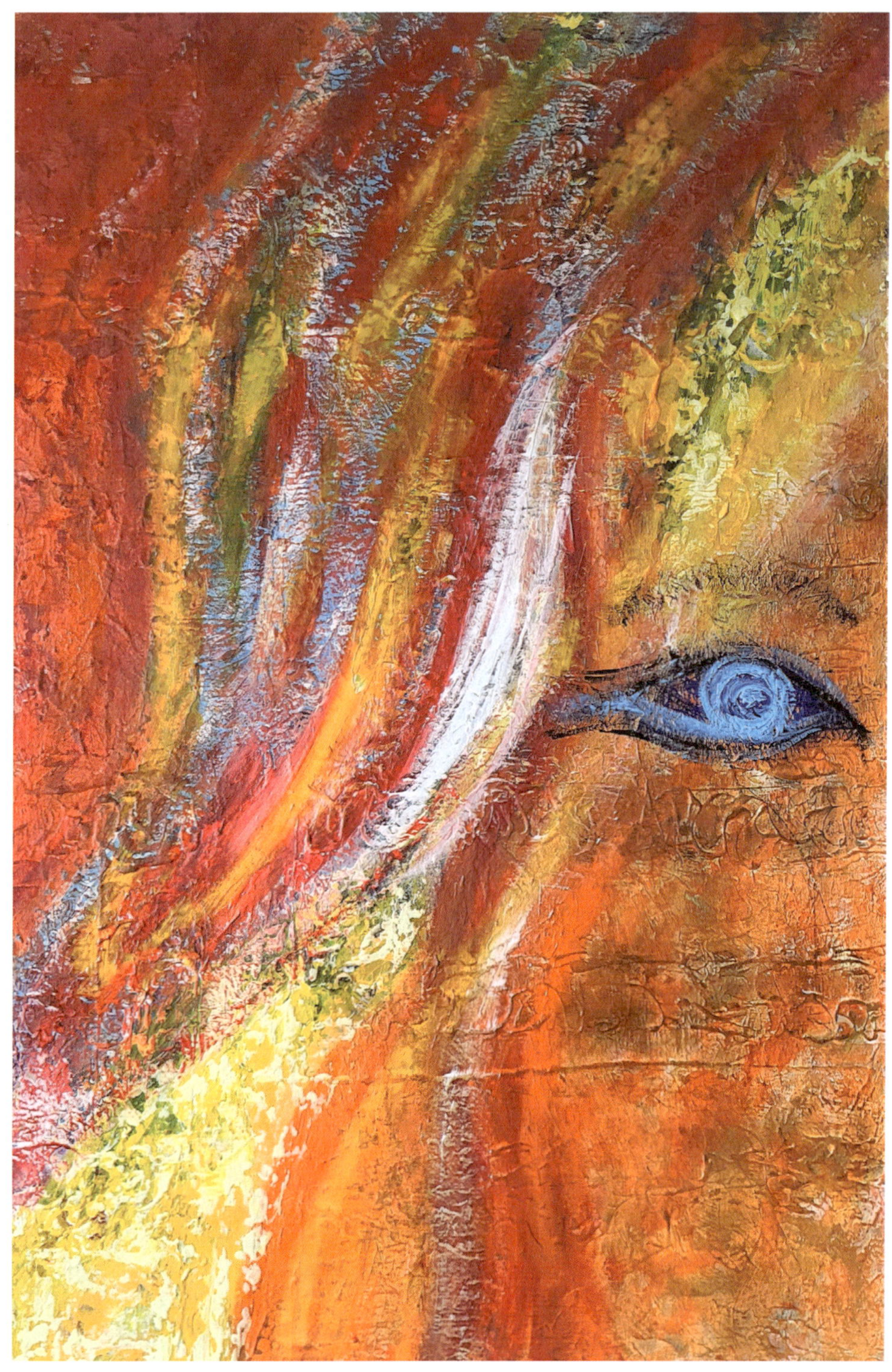

I see you

Acrylic on canvas, 2021
4 x 2 ¹/₂ feet

THE CALL

ALIGNING HEART AND SPIRIT

In the following personal examples, I share how I was called to connect with Spirit and begin living a life aligned with my heart.

Meditation

In March 2020, I began having persistent **thoughts** to meditate for 30 days. I could not understand why this was happening as I was not someone who meditated.

These **thoughts** continued almost daily from March to mid–May 2020. They were so relentless that I made a commitment to follow through during all of June. The first three weeks were extremely emotional and I broke down in tears every day. I felt deep-rooted loss, despair, frustration, anger, anxiety and fear—feelings associated with my childhood. In meditation, I made every effort to fully embrace all emotions and as the month wore on, sessions became less emotional.

I only managed to do 27 days out of 30. Considering this was my first major commitment to meditation, I felt I had done well. But because the first three weeks were so intense, on some days I was too exhausted to meditate. And that concluded my initial call to connect with Spirit.

Creative expression

After completing my first journey in meditation, I decided to commit to practising it twice a week. In one session near the end of July 2020, I **thought** I should take up painting. Like the previous **thoughts** to meditate for 30 days, these new ones persisted with intensity into September 2020. It was only at this point that I decided to *listen*. After scoping out what art supplies were available in my community, I decided that I wanted to paint on large canvases and asked a friend to build me three 5 x 3-foot frames.

I was excited about moving in this new direction; yet, after bringing the frames home, I let them sit on my kitchen floor for a month. **Thoughts** to stretch the canvas and begin to paint emerged daily, but again I ignored them.

By early October 2020, these **thoughts** intensified. Once again, it took me a while to *listen*. In fact, it took me three months to implement the **thought** and start painting. On October 18, 2020 I finally put brush to canvas. I specifically remember the feelings of newness and uncertainty brewing with excitement. It meant crossing a line into a new space.

Thoughts: *represent communications from heart space/Spirit. They are subtle and can be persistent.*

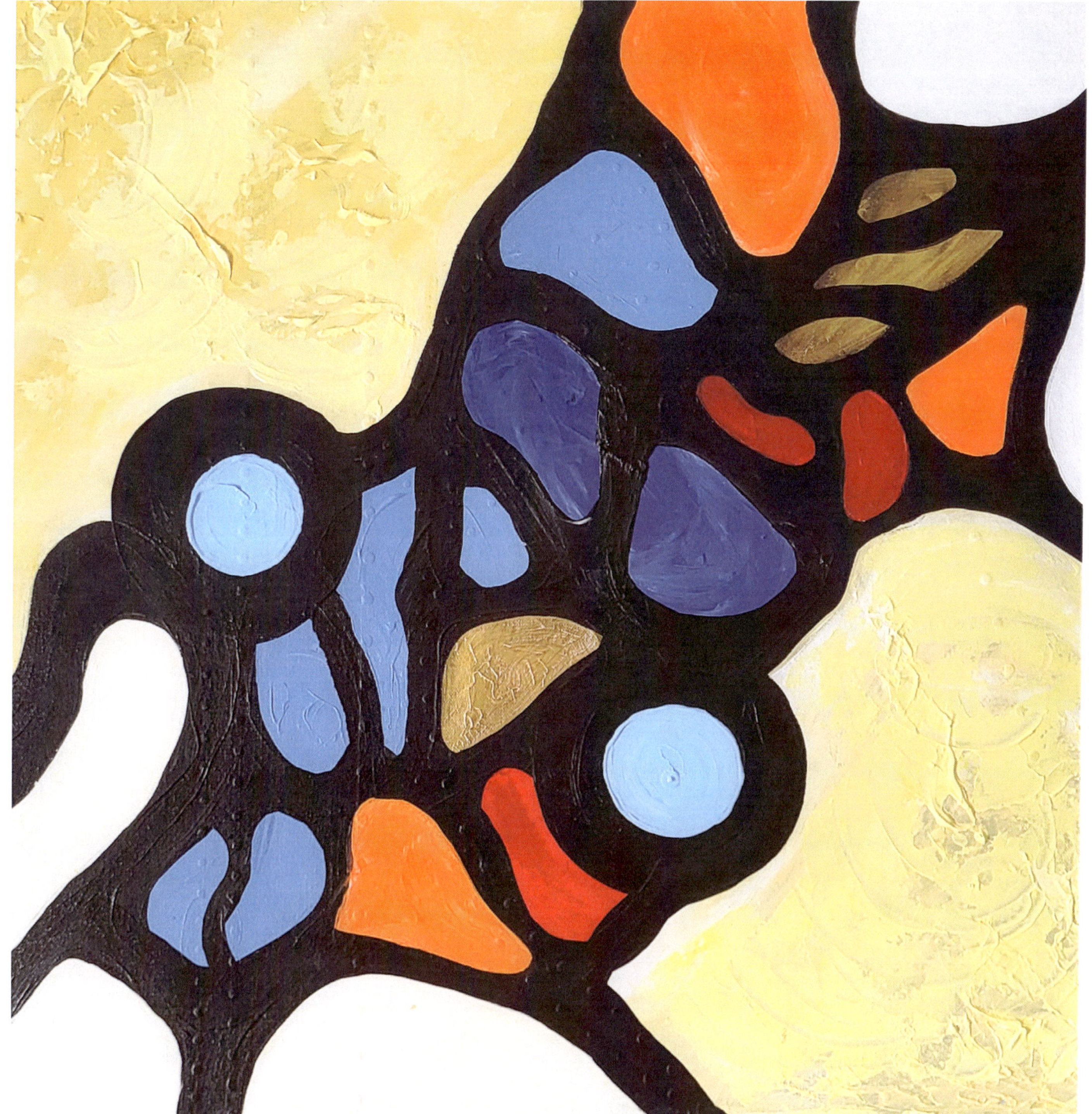

Attraction 2

Acrylic on canvas, 2024

2 x 2 feet

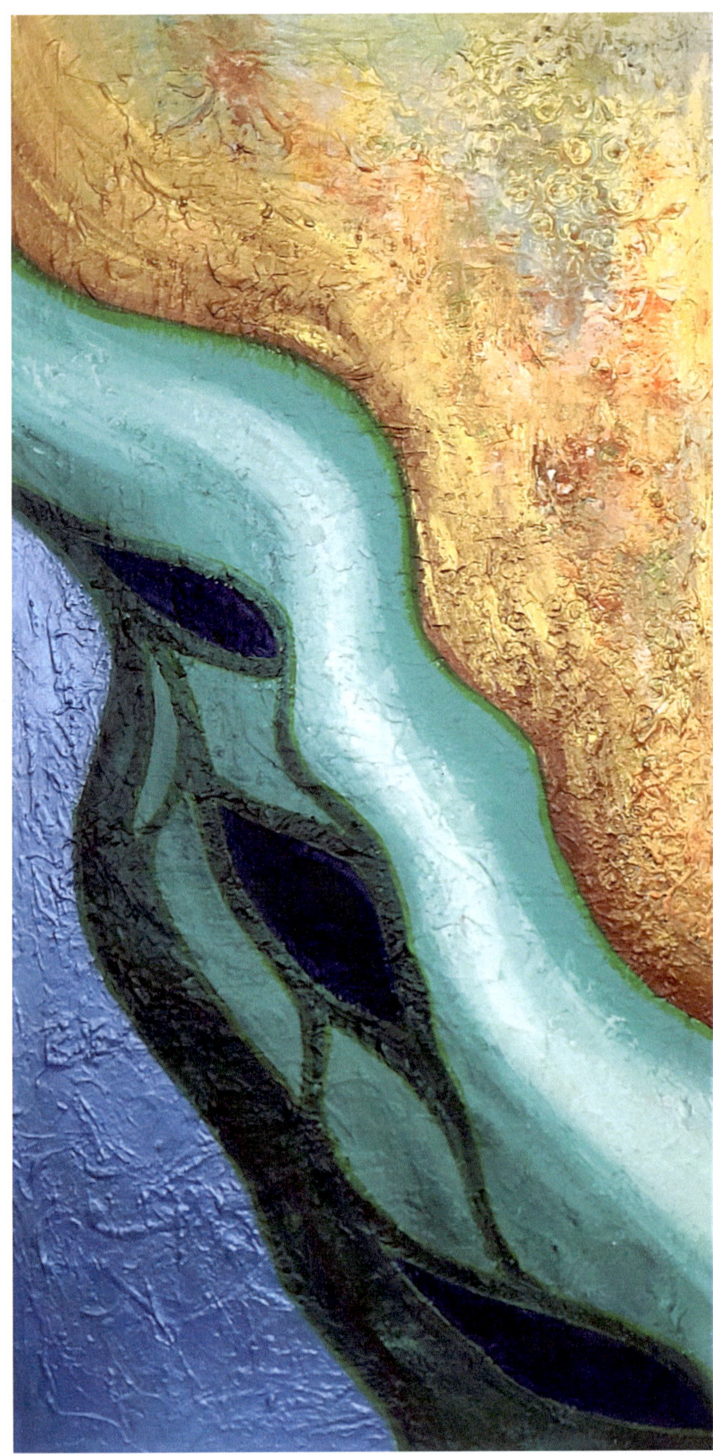

Strength

Acrylic on canvas, 2021
4 x 2 feet

Willingness to learn

Learning something new can be daunting, but you never know what will bring out the best in you until you try. I certainly never thought I would become an abstract artist, nor did I think I would write a book on meditation, art and spirituality.

I did not receive any formal education in abstract painting. I relied on YouTube videos to teach me how to stretch canvas, texturize and mix colours. And I followed my instincts.

In the beginning, I tried to paint an image of a moosehide stretched on a wooden frame. But I felt as though I were painting immaturely like a child, so I rolled up the canvas and stored it. Feeling self-conscious and critical, I then initiated **thoughts** to approach painting abstractly with no expectations, allowing my brush or palette knife to flow without much thought. This became a meditative state in which I painted whatever came to me.

My style has shifted from free-flowing to experimental with stylized faces and geometry. I admit there is something interesting about painting geometric shapes that makes me feel not only calm but also focused. I decided to use geometric painting to problem-solve issues, incorporating forms of geometric design into my strategic planning process for work and overall life.

Earth and fire

Acrylic on canvas, 2022
4 x 2 ¹/₂ feet

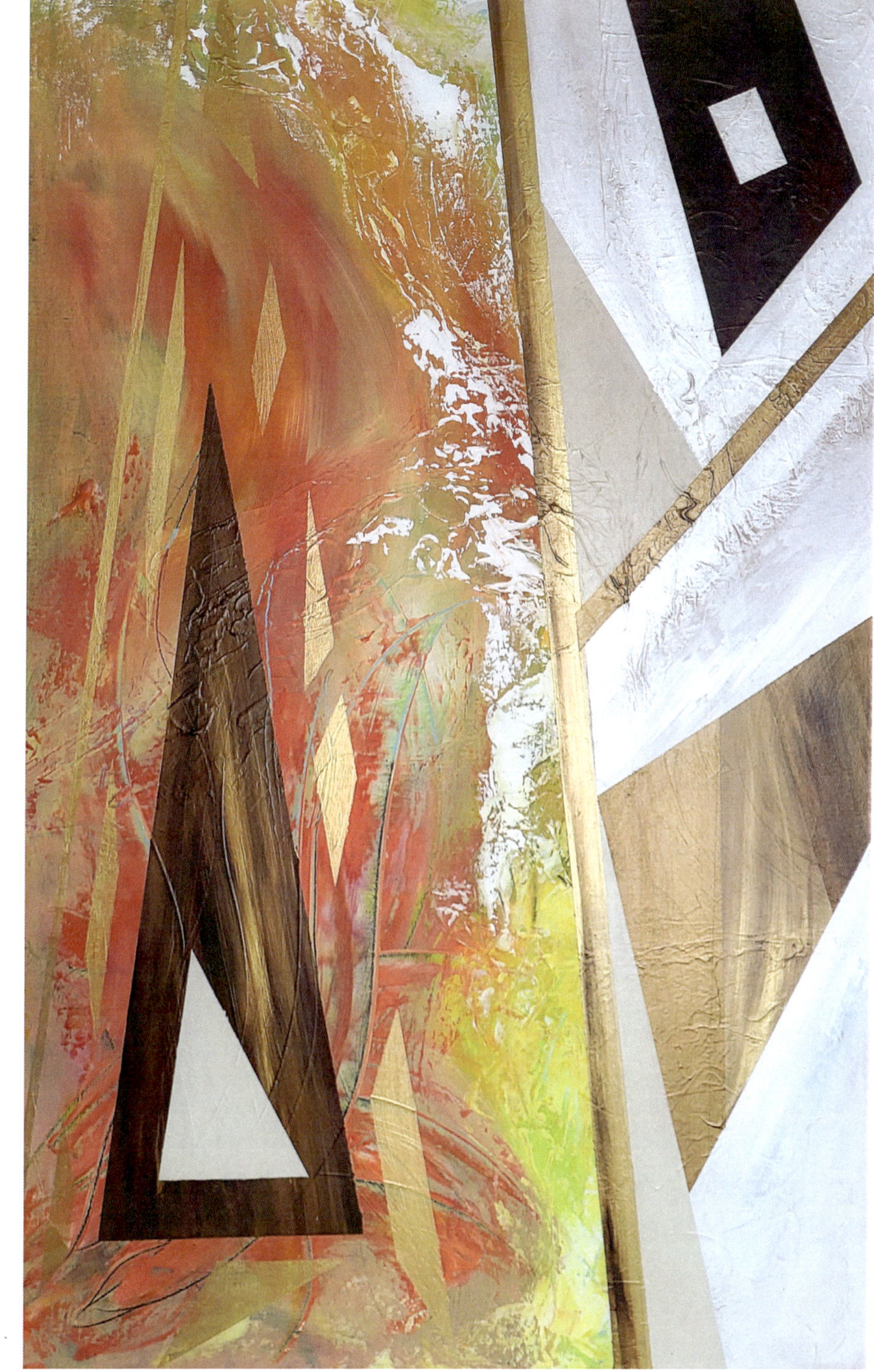

Awareness and strategy

With so many micro and macro events and situations competing on a personal, local, national and global level, I felt pulled in many directions. I had **thoughts** to take time out for myself, to take stock and reflect.

In my reflection, I asked myself questions such as:

- To what am I giving attention?
- To whom am I giving attention?
- What insecurities come up?
- Where am I doing too much or too little?
- What and whom am I hanging onto unnecessarily?
- Do the people around me improve my well-being?
- Am I supported, valued and respected?
- Am I resisting change?

Self-reflection offered me a space to think more strategically about the direction of my life and what I would like to see and experience. Once my blockages were cleared, I was in a better position to adjust my environment to harmonize with my true essence.

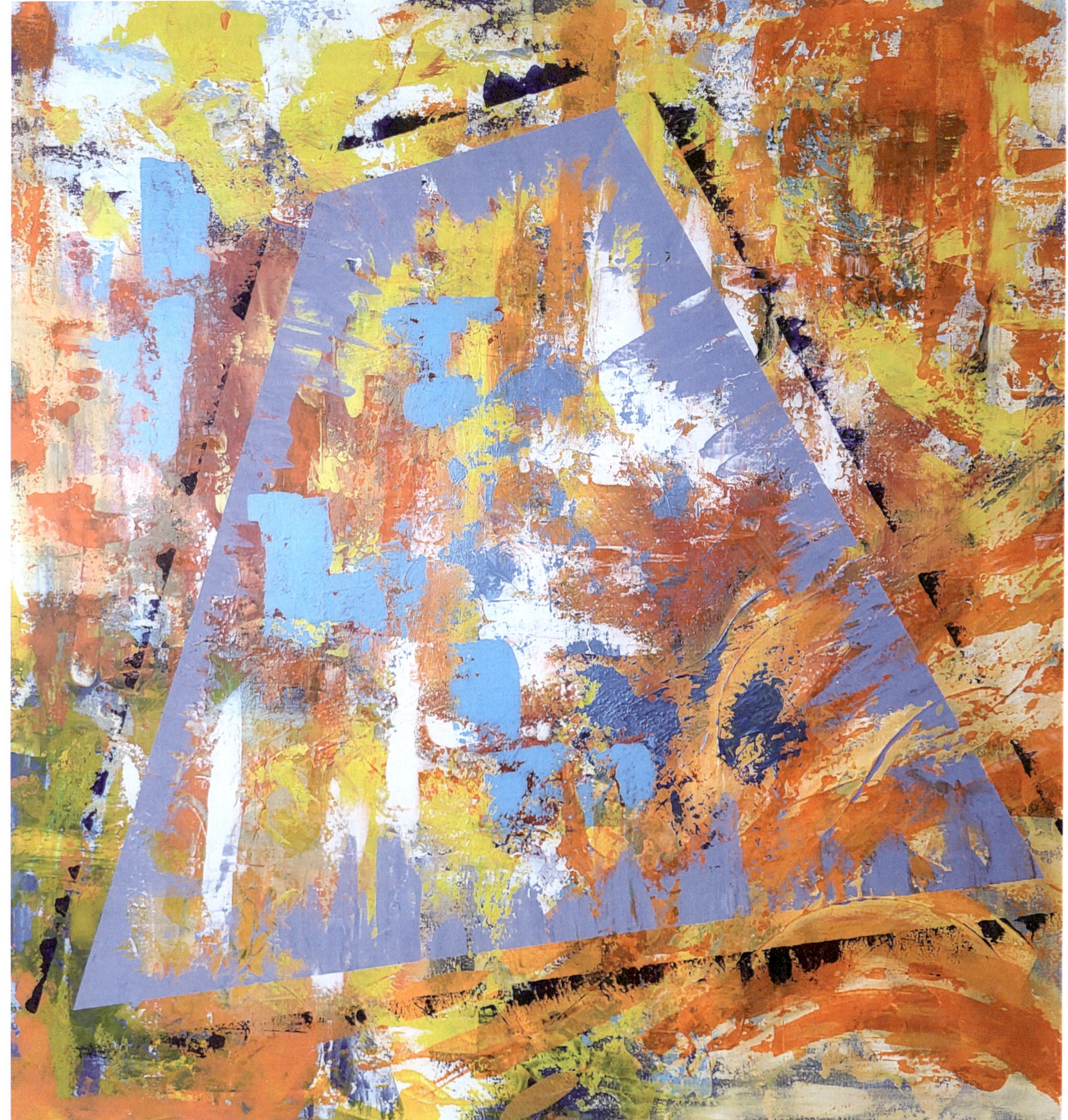

*Gateway to
a new you*

Acrylic on canvas, 2022
4 x 4 feet

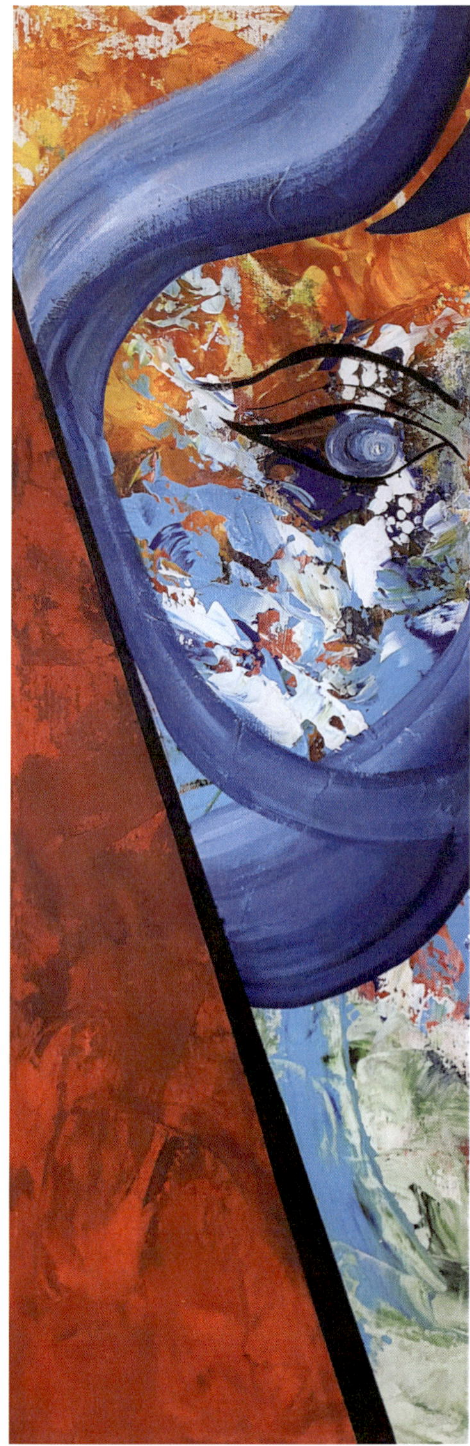

I AM GUIDED.

Seer

Acrylic on canvas, 2021
3 x 1 feet

Letting go through art

In April 2021, my **thoughts** turned toward painting with a therapeutic lens. This meant working on a specific issue that had plagued me throughout my life: my sense of self-worth.

I started out with one canvas that I intentionally painted to transform any negative feelings around this topic. With each layer of paint, I deliberately shaped and changed my feelings around a lack of worthiness. It was a gradual process over three months, done in silence.

During this time, I began to notice a shift in my interactions with certain people, particularly those with whom the dynamic was one-sided or insincere. Gradually, I redefined my landscape of people, identifying those who were true friends and supporters and others who were not. At the end of this challenging but worthwhile period, I concluded that I had the power to choose the occupants of my space.

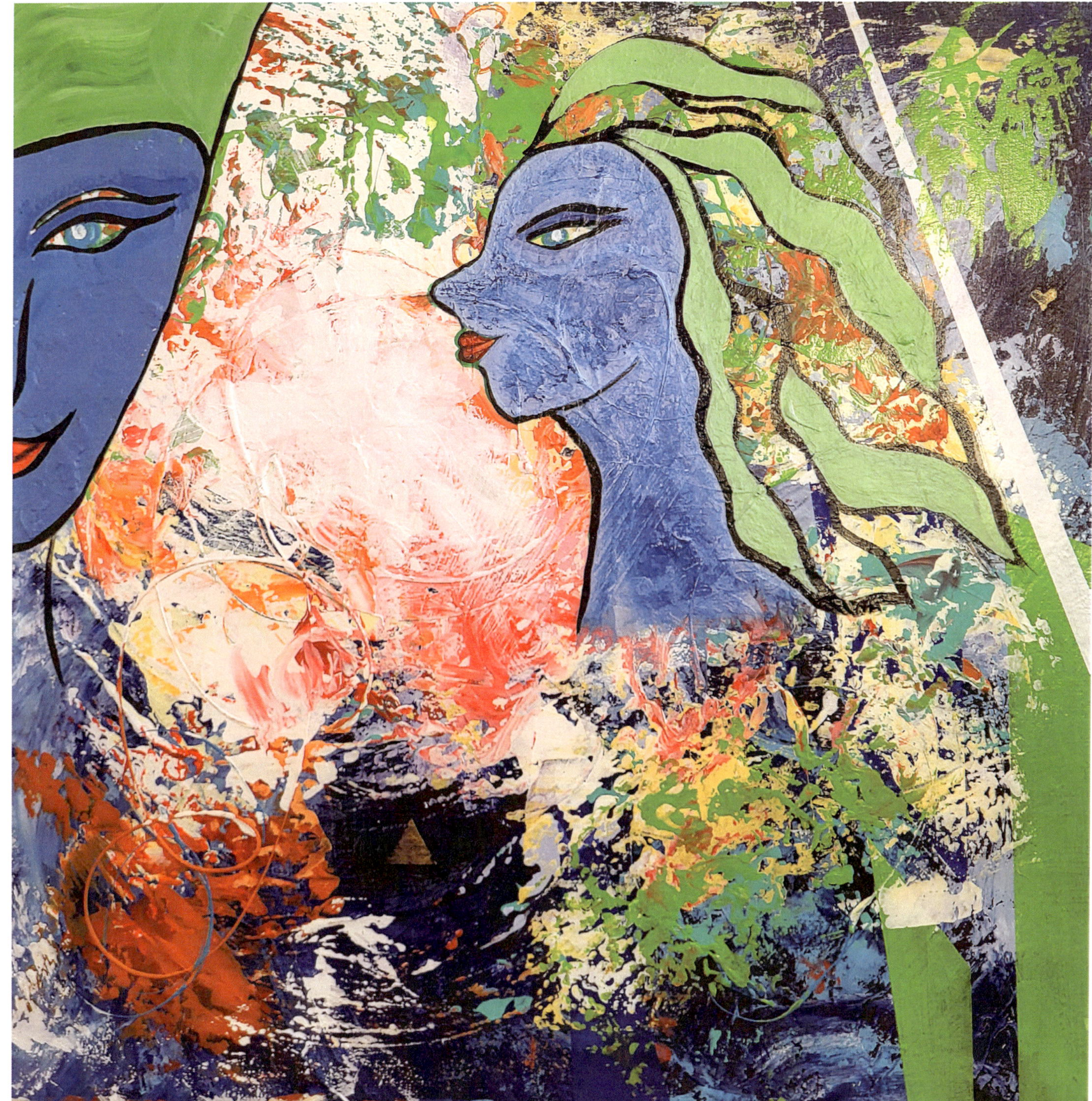

Relations

Acrylic on canvas, 2022
2 x 2 feet

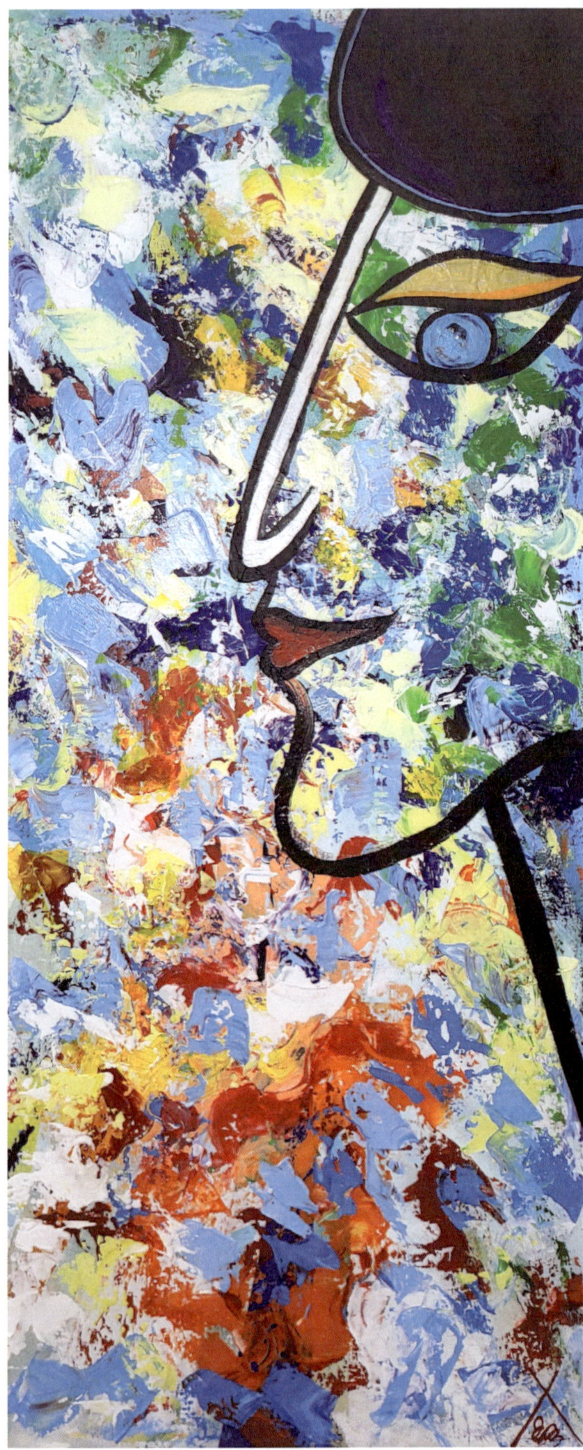

Ask for help

Acrylic on canvas, 2022
5 x 2 feet

Asking for help

Working through my sense of self-worth, I started having **thoughts** about new career opportunities. I wanted an occupation that was meaningful and a workplace where colleagues were amazing change-makers —not complacent or satisfied with maintaining the status quo. I wanted to see fairness and inclusion of Indigenous Peoples in project planning. A place where Indigenous employees contributed to discussions in a meaningful way.

In my May 2021 meditations, I asked my Spirit guides for help. Their response was to repeat to myself: "I am being presented with amazing career-enhancing opportunities." I reiterated this message to myself while engaging in activities such as walking, dishwashing and painting.

Three months later, I began receiving invitations to job interviews. By October, I had a couple of job offers, chose one and embarked on a new journey.

My desire to embrace new career possibilities continues. It did not stop once I accepted a new job.

Dreaming big

Committing to heart/Spirit

In December 2021, I **thought** about meditating for 90 days. I decided to *listen* and committed to starting on January 2, 2022. However, **thoughts** to begin earlier emerged, so I started on December 28, 2021 and ended successfully on March 27, 2022. As the final day approached, I decided to maintain a daily meditation schedule, and did not break that commitment until September when I went camping with friends on Great Slave Lake.

Three days into my 90-day meditation, I had **thoughts** to pay attention to the energy within my body, but in relation to my overall *thinking* patterns. It was a challenge in the beginning but once I became attuned, it was a great eye-opener. I found myself questioning what caught my attention, and was able to recognize my body's reaction to my environment and the people in it. For example, I found my muscles tensing around certain people.

This experience raised awareness of my approach to life and confirmed that for my personal health, I must incorporate meditation into my daily life.

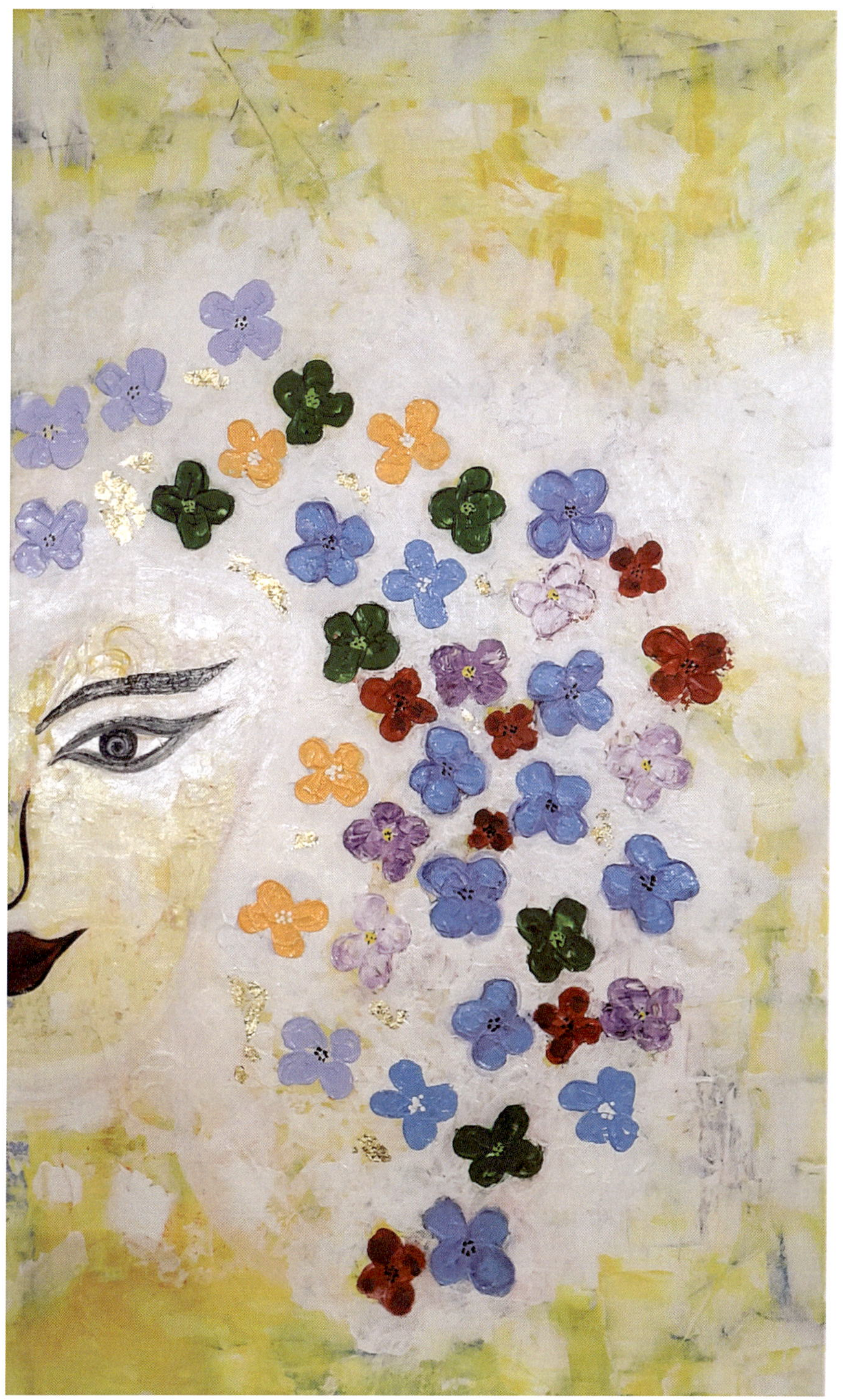

Trust

Acrylic on board, 2023
5 x 3 feet

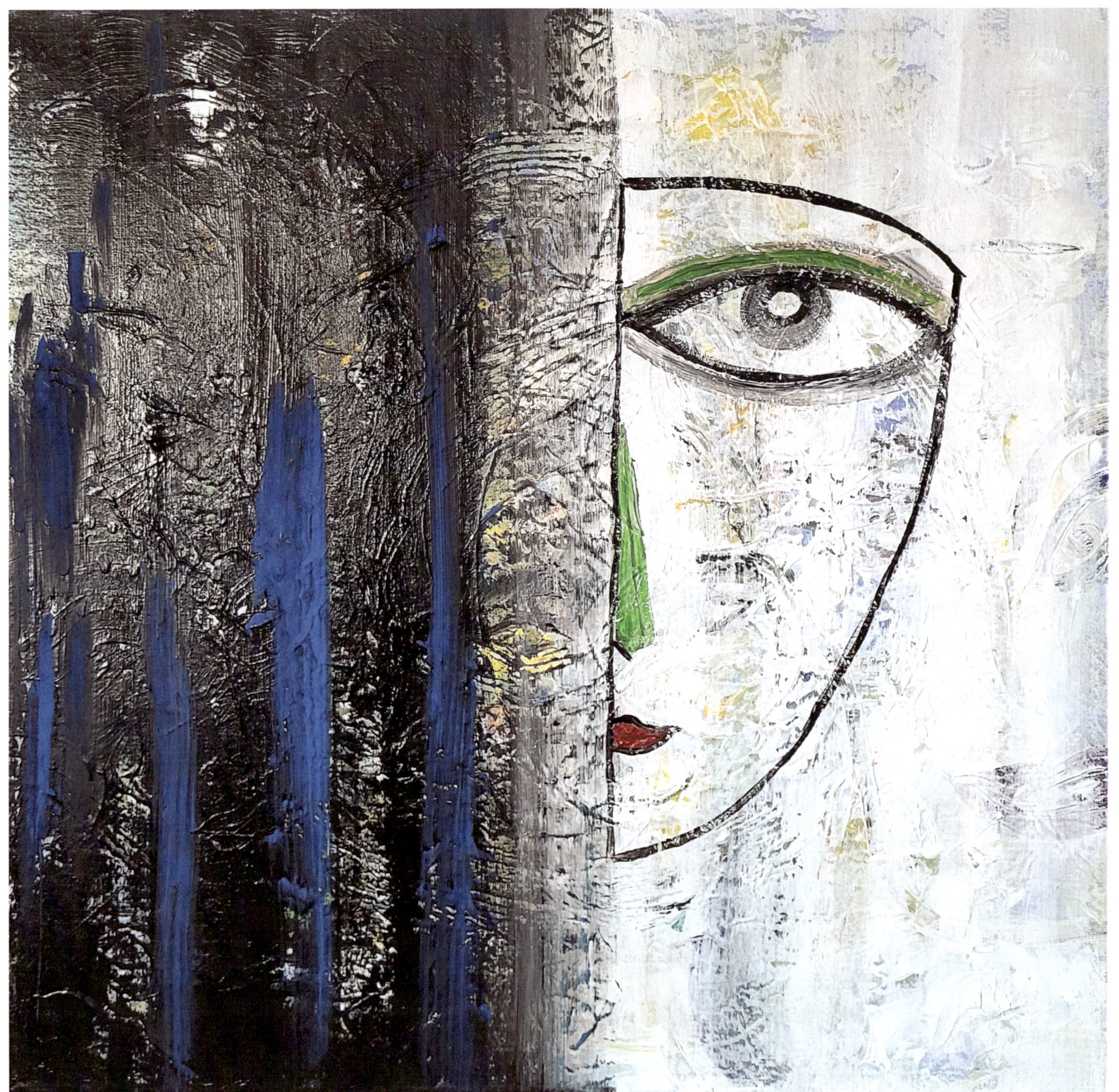

I AM WAITING.

Spirit

Acrylic on canvas, 2023
2 x 2 feet

The door to empowerment

Acrylic on canvas, 2023
4 x 3 feet

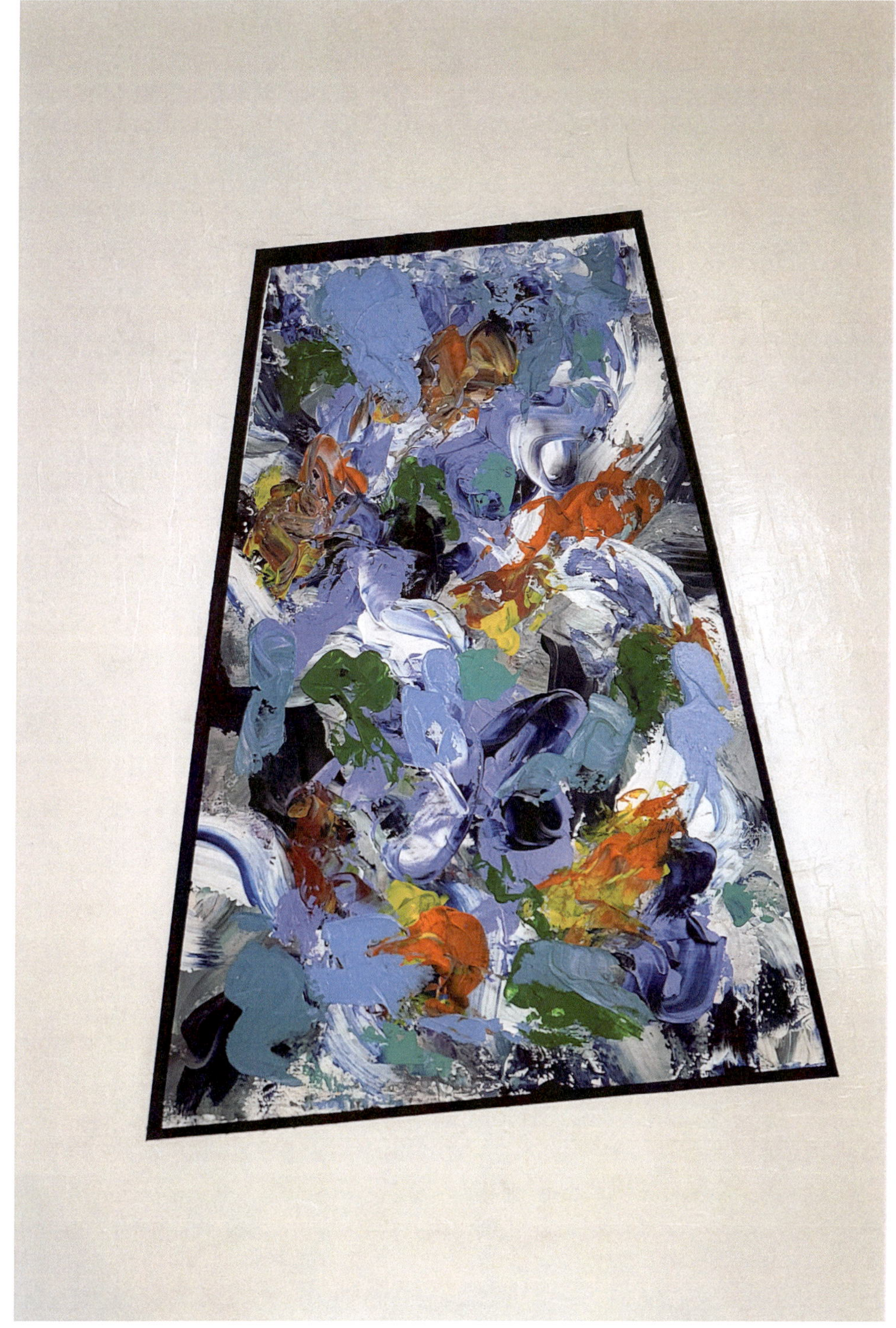

Strategic divine guidance

In December 2021, I had **thoughts** of organizing a private art show at my place for friends and acquaintances. I followed through and after much positive feedback, my ego rose a few notches. I started to *think* about the possibility of organizing an art show in Vancouver in the summer of 2022. However, I had no idea how to do this.

During this period, I was telling friends and anyone who would listen that I wanted to do an art showing in Vancouver in July of 2022. By the end of January, I started to have **thoughts** that I should "check in" through meditation to see if that was what I should really be focusing on. I remember feeling as if I were "being told." I **thought** I should not allow my ego to run wild after one little art show.

At first, I ignored these **thoughts** and did not check in. But they persisted until I acted on them. In early February, I finally decided to meditate and ask if the Vancouver Art Fair was right for me.

As I settled into meditation, I mentally declared the following to my Spirit guides: "You wanted me to begin meditating; I did it. You wanted me to start painting; I did it. Now what do you want me to do with my artwork?" To my surprise, I immediately saw

a book—this book. I discerned that I could explain in pictures and words how I was guided to connect with my heart/Spirit. As soon as I envisioned the book, I asked "How do I do this?" The **thought** that emerged was: "Call Kathryn; she knows."

I was quite taken aback by this experience, because leading up to this point, I felt these **thoughts** were coming only from my heart. But I started to think there was something more going on since the impressions and/or **thoughts** were so clear that I felt I was talking to someone or something.

I called Kathryn to chat about my meditation experience and to see whether she knew how I could begin the process of creating a book. Fortunately, someone close to her had just published a book with photos so she was able to provide details of the process and send me a link to the platform used to create their book.

This experience truly increased my connection with heart/Spirit. My relationship with the guides was evolving; they were becoming advisors.

I began writing the original version of this book in late February 2022 after persistent **thoughts** to get on with it. By the end of March, I had ordered three copies of my first draft to be printed in hardcover.

When the books arrived in early May, I was quite pleased with and proud of what I had accomplished. I would not have come to this point had I not *listened* to my spiritual guides.

Two weeks after receiving those first books, I meditated and asked for guidance on logistics for proceeding. I wondered if I should self-publish on Amazon or find a publisher. My initial **thought** was that I would eventually meet someone who would provide direction.

Five months later, I was surprised to receive an invitation to a public meeting, where a conversation with another participant yielded an introduction to a friend who had issued several books on Amazon.

After I explained my book idea and its history to that author, he advised that I go through a publisher. He also identified one whose sole focus was books about art and spirituality.

And I realized the door had just opened. I was feeling very impressed with my spiritual guides, and my trust in their guidance had risen to new levels.

I AM MYSTERIOUS.

Blue light

Acrylic on canvas, 2020
3 x 2 feet

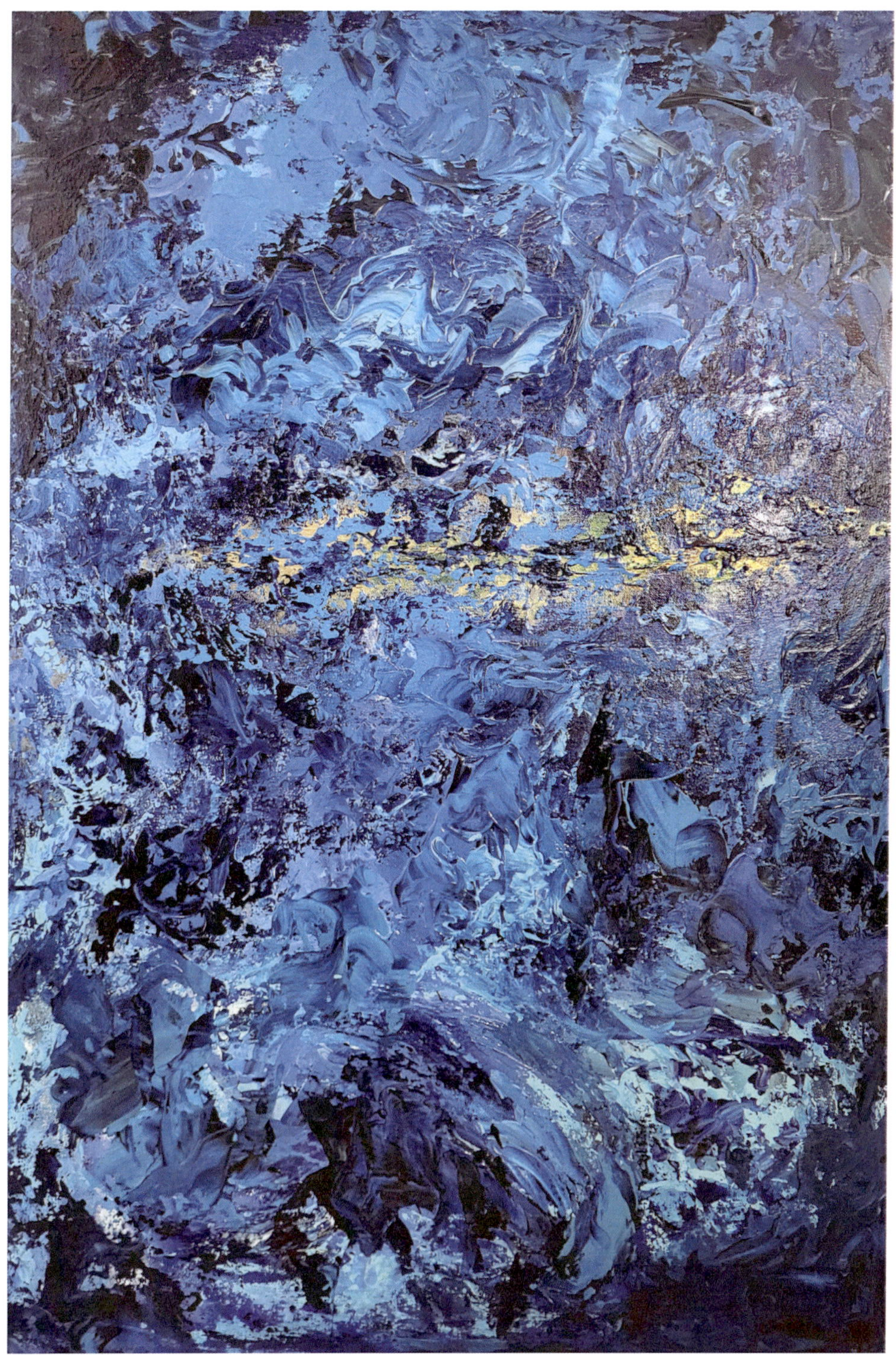

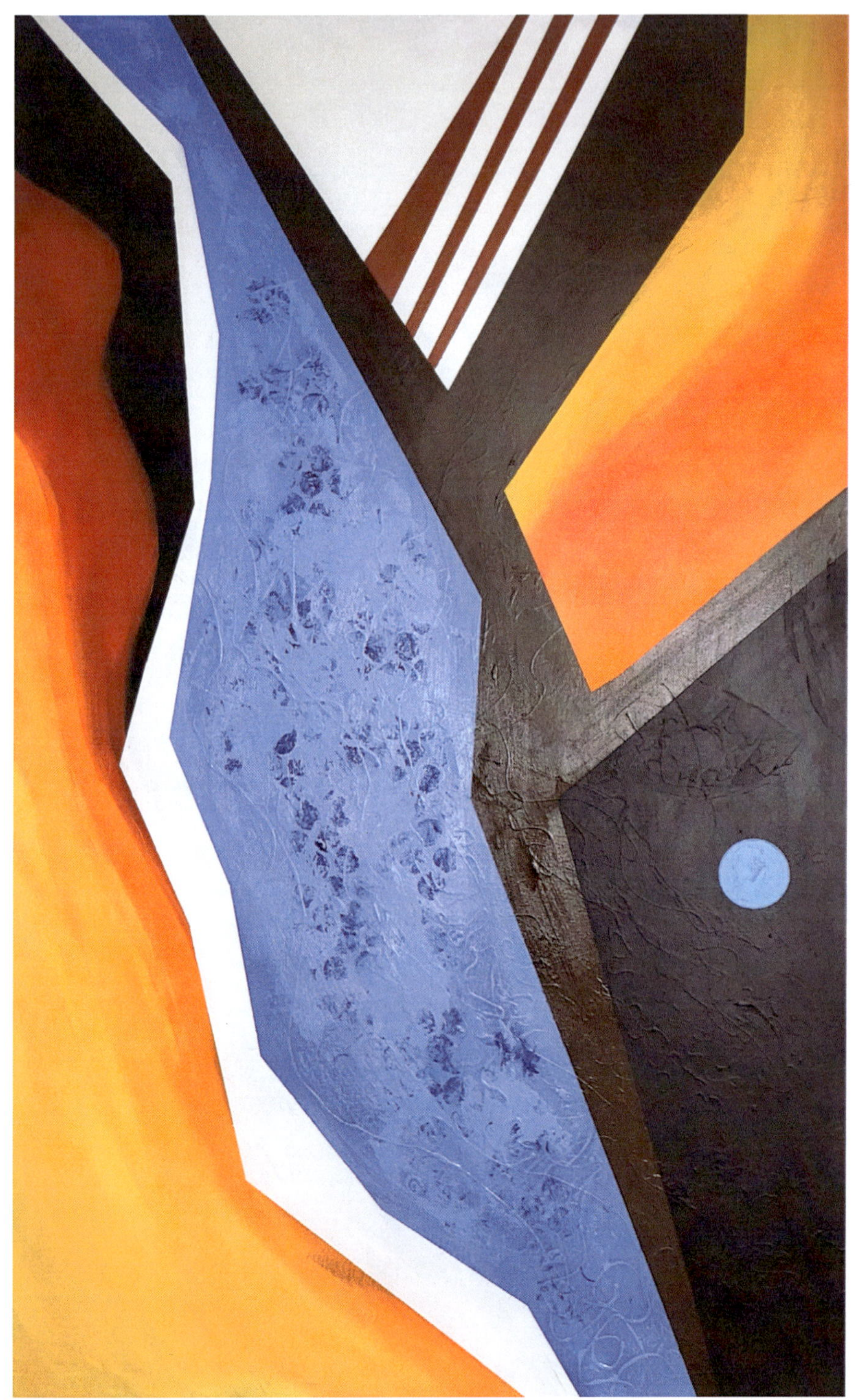

I love you

Acrylic on canvas, 2024
5 x 3 feet

SPIRITUALITY AND A NEW LIFE

Letting go of the negatives; focusing on the positives

I hope these personal examples illustrate how Spirit communicated with me through subtle thoughts. When I ignored them, they became very insistent, like a child tugging at my sleeve for attention. I want to make it very clear that Spirit will never tell you to hurt yourself or others. It operates for our highest good and the highest good of others.

Strategically, Spirit guided me through the process of surrendering a way of being that suppressed what was innately in me. I started by committing to heed its guidance, incorporate meditation into my daily habits and trust that it had my best interests in mind.

Acknowledging my spiritual identity has been life-changing. However, I want to stress that just because I recognized it does not mean that I'm automatically spiritual forever. It's a way of being that I know requires commitment to maintain. The things that I found challenging in the past may still come up, but I now see them through a new set of eyes. I am making intentional choices and defining the parameters within which I am willing to work.

The people and circumstances that jarred me in the past no longer take up significant real estate in my head. In fact, I am in the process of rezoning the regulations to a much more enticing category—one of love and creativity.

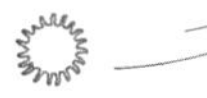

If I work at this, what else can I discover?

—Eileen Marlowe

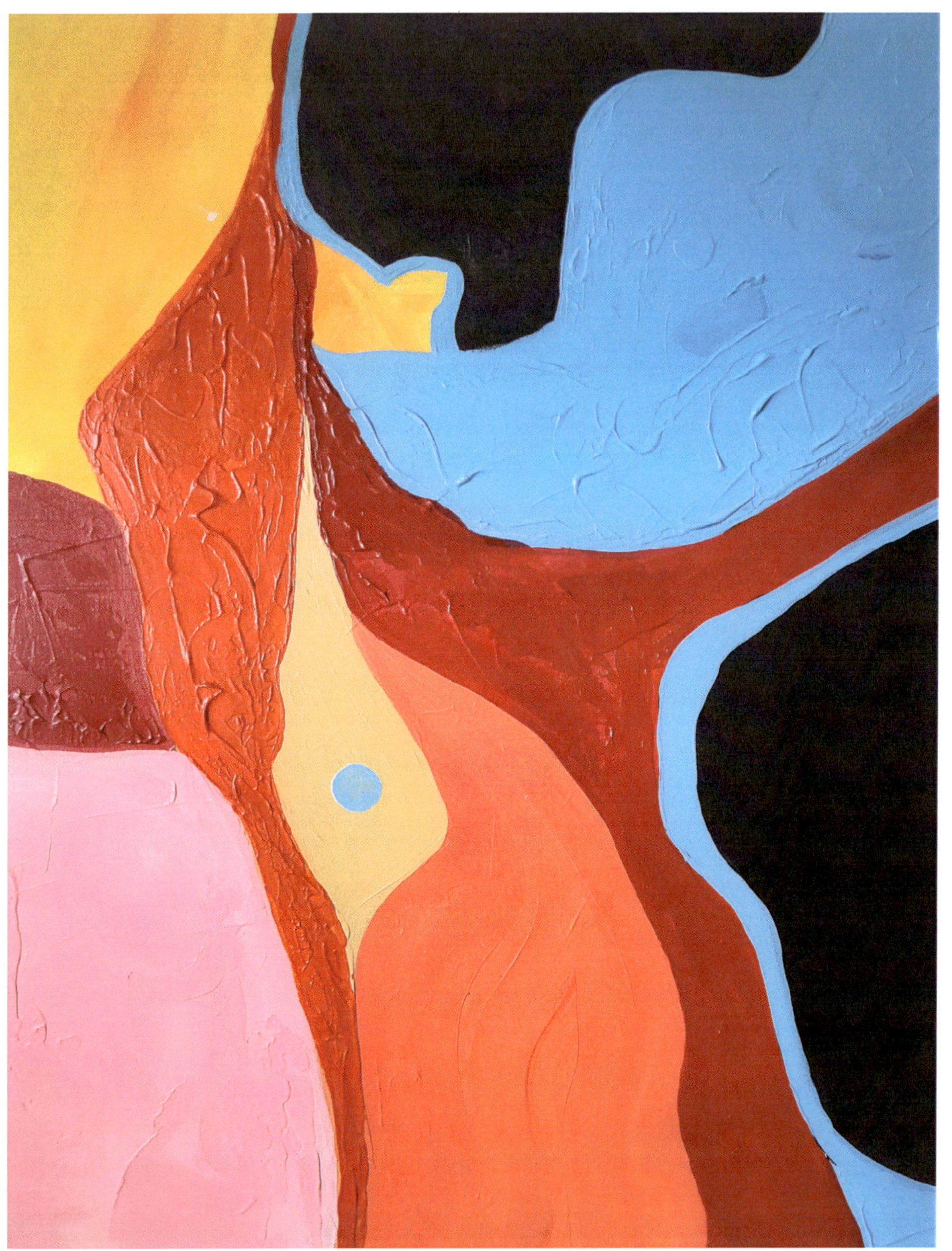

Focus

Acrylic on canvas, 2022
4 x 3 feet

BENEFITS OF FOCUSING ON MY HEART IN MEDITATION

Designing the future

Focusing on my heart during meditation provided me with several benefits:

- I released the "heavy and stuck" energy within me and aligned myself with creativity to approach my life with meaning.

- I took up abstract painting and made it a permanent part of my life. The act of painting brought out a sense of love and joy in me—something that had been missing.

- Focusing on my heart gave me the opportunity to re-examine my life and chart a path forward in a meaningful manner.

- I now embrace the strength within me without feeling that I need to minimize myself for the comfort of others.

- I recognize fear and ego as barriers to acknowledging my spiritual identity.

- I now treat ill-intentioned people as a reminder to love myself.

- I acknowledge my spiritual identity and have made *listening* to my spiritual guides a priority. I no longer ignore them to the extent that I did.

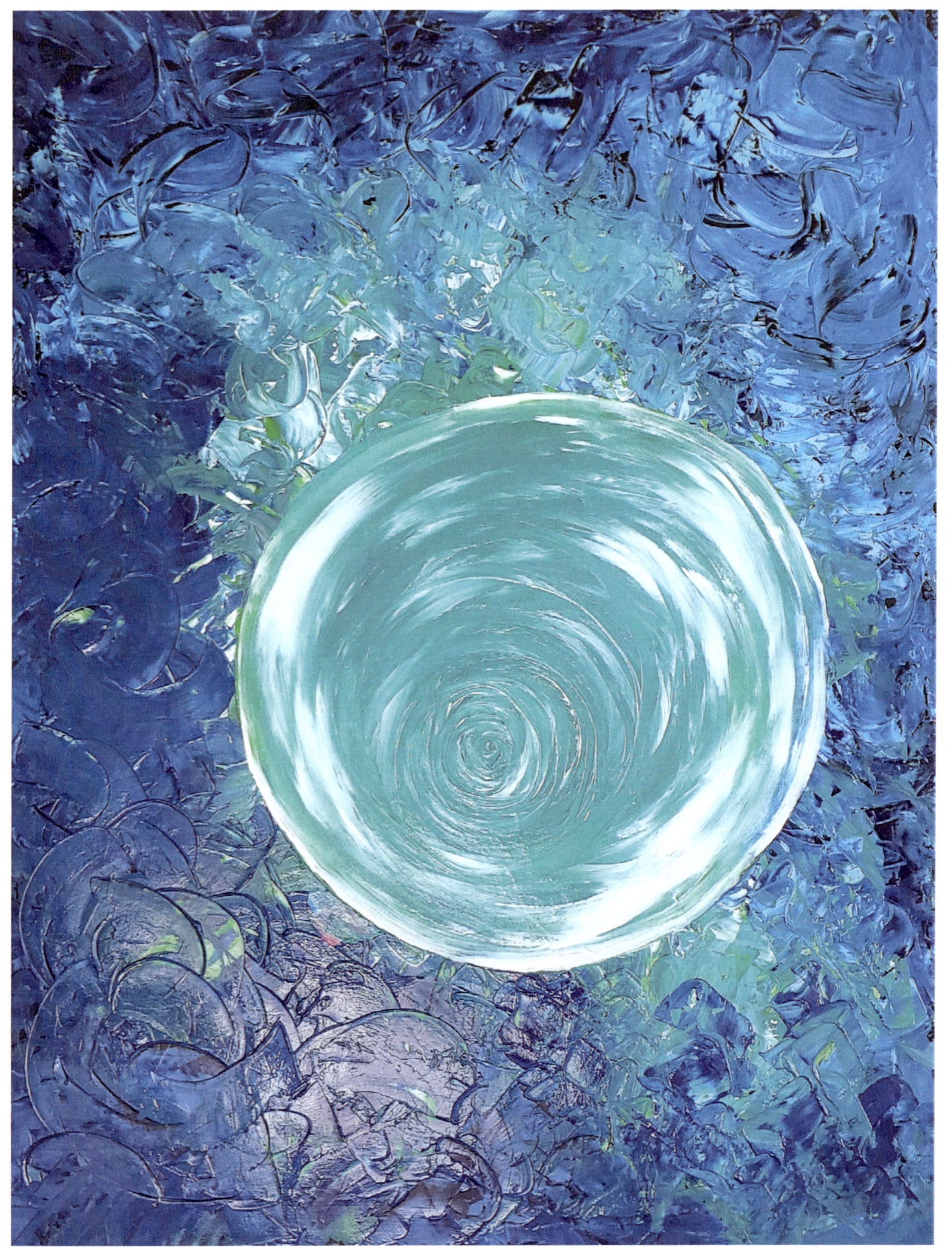

Going within

Acrylic on canvas, 2021
4 x 3 feet

PROCESS OF OPENING MY HEART TO SPIRIT

Setting the stage for a clean break

1) SELF-ASSESSED AND CLEARED AWAY BLOCKAGES

To learn the language of the heart/Spirit, I had to first embrace the things I found difficult. This meant taking stock of my life and asking some hard questions:

- Am I running uphill or downhill?

- What have I been avoiding?

- Under what conditions do I tend to settle?

- What have I been telling myself?

- What patterns do I need to let go of?

- And what do I want?

I had to set the stage to make myself a priority. Metaphorically, I cleaned my house, reorganized, decluttered and refreshed.

Embarking on this journey was difficult emotionally and mentally. I took a break from or eliminated interactions with people in my life such as those who did not respect me or put me on the back burner at their convenience.

2) MADE MEDITATION A DAILY PRACTICE

Once I took stock and cleared away the blockages, I was in a better place to sit in daily meditation without too much distraction.

3) MADE SELF-AWARENESS A PRIORITY

To learn the language of my heart/Spirit, I had to practise self-awareness. I needed to become aware of my thoughts and how my body responded to people and environments. I also had to distinguish between my headspace/brain/ego decisions and Spirit-driven outcomes through my heart space.

Self-awareness played an integral role in my efforts to understand how my heart/Spirit communicates. I conducted a self-awareness exercise in collaboration with meditation over a 90-day period. It was not easy at first but was incredibly rewarding because I learned so much about myself and about how my body reacts to the people around me. It was an eye-opening experience.

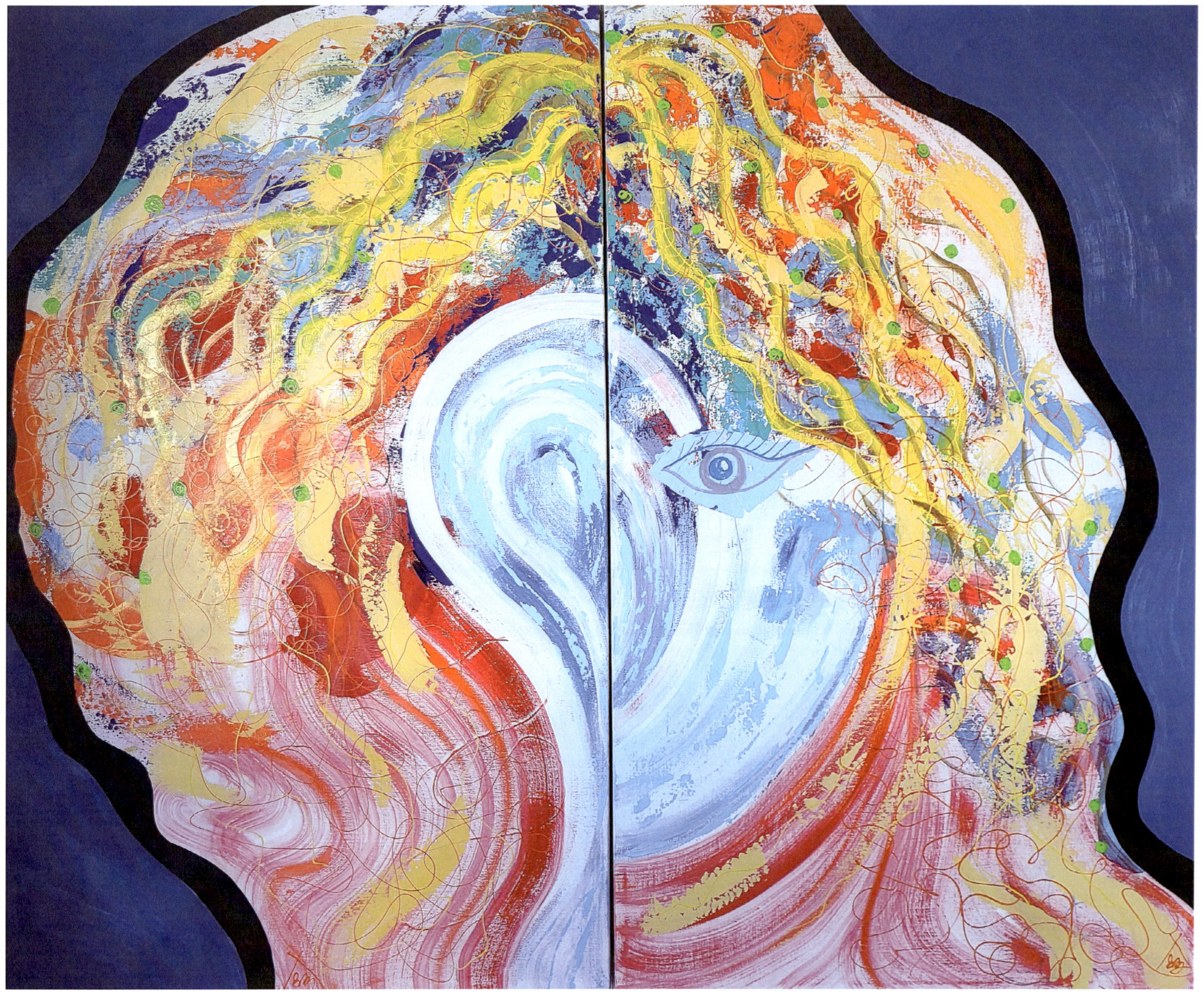

WHAT I HAVE LEARNED

Lessons from experience

These personal experiences have taught me that spirituality emanates directly from extraterrestrial beings. I acknowledge that I have much more to learn, but here are my initial findings so far:

- Communications between my headspace/brain (ego) and my heart/Spirit are very different.

- Ego and repressed emotions cloud communications with my spiritual guides.

- The disconnection I had felt all my life emanated from a failure to acknowledge my spiritual identity.

- Persistent **thoughts** are a call from my spiritual guides.

- My spiritual guides communicate with me through the heart.

- My heart/Spirit provides access to a system of intelligence.

- A healthy mind and body are needed to understand the language of the heart/Spirit.

- My spiritual guides are loving and want to help me.

- My spiritual guidance comes from a place that considers the highest good for me and those around me.

- Spirituality is a practice that must be maintained.

- I am a "powerhouse." I recognize I have a strong presence. I fully embrace it without fearing ridicule for being who I am.

- My formal education did not consider what sits in my heart.

- All relationships have an expiration date.

- Holding onto people and situations longer than necessary stunts my personal growth.

I AM BEAUTIFUL.

Self-awareness

Acrylic on canvas, 2023
2 panels, 5 x 3 feet

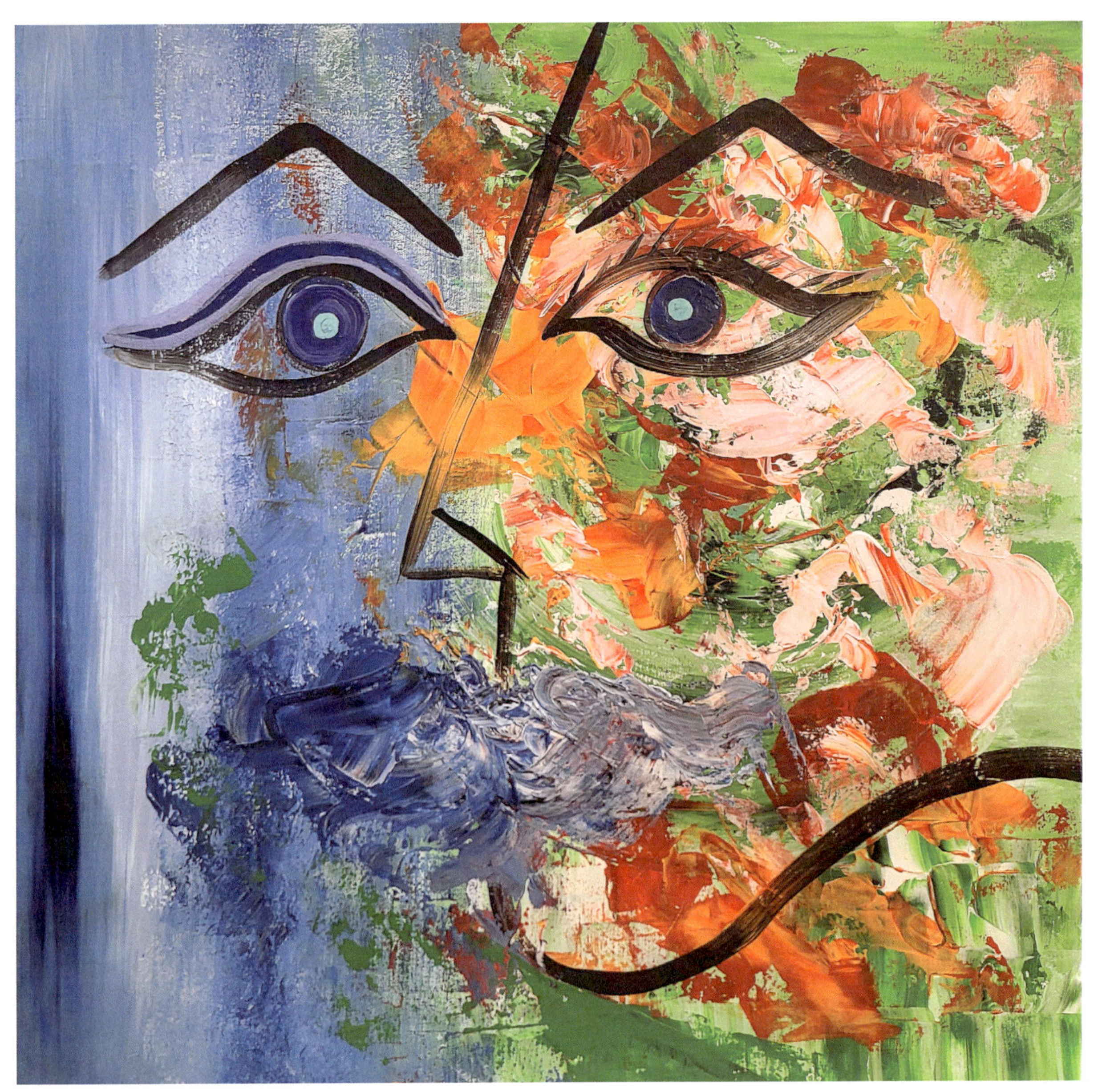

*I am the designer
of my life*

Acrylic on canvas, 2023
2 x 2 feet

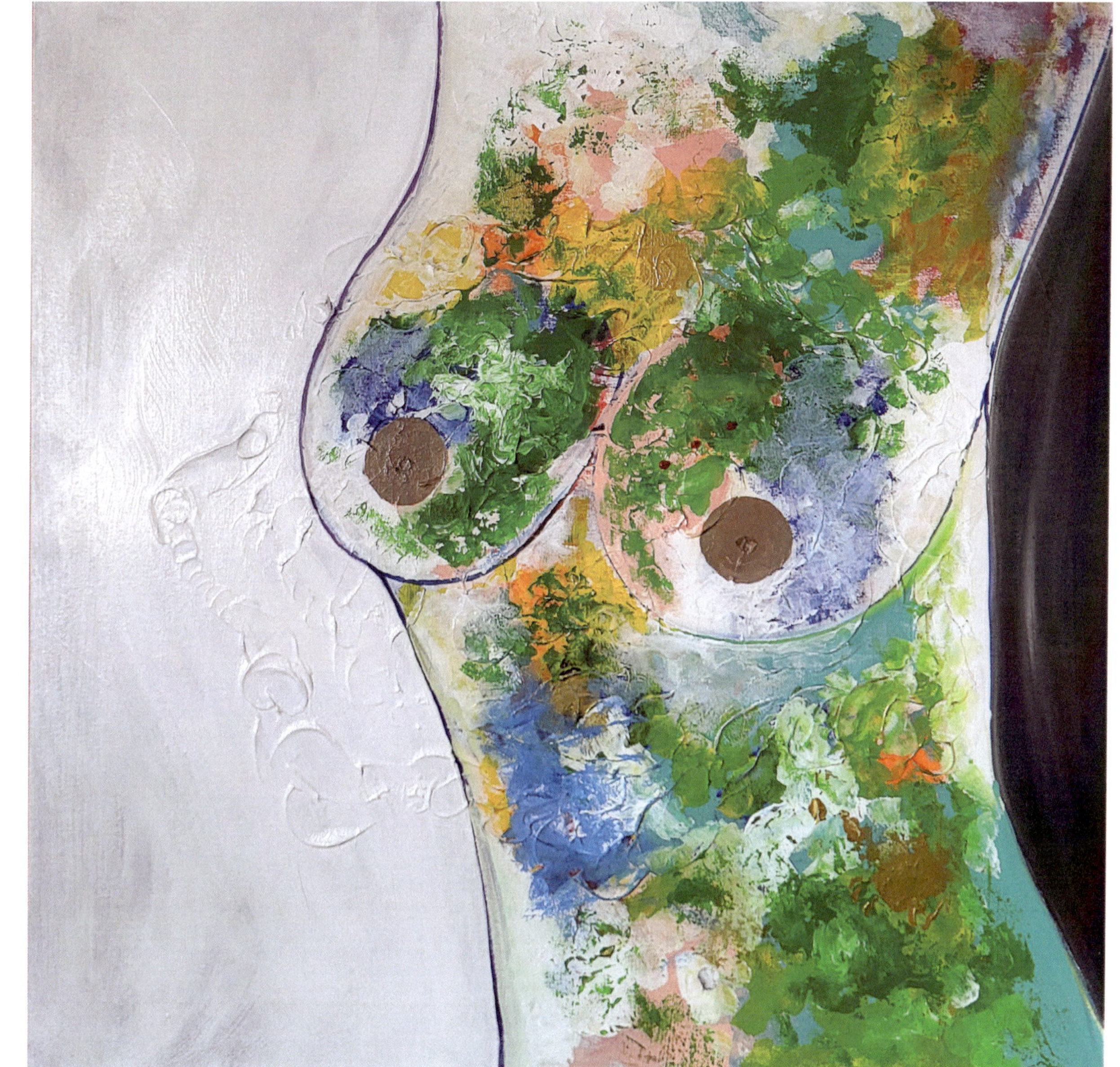

I AM ENERGY.

Love me

Acrylic on canvas, 2023
2 x 2 feet

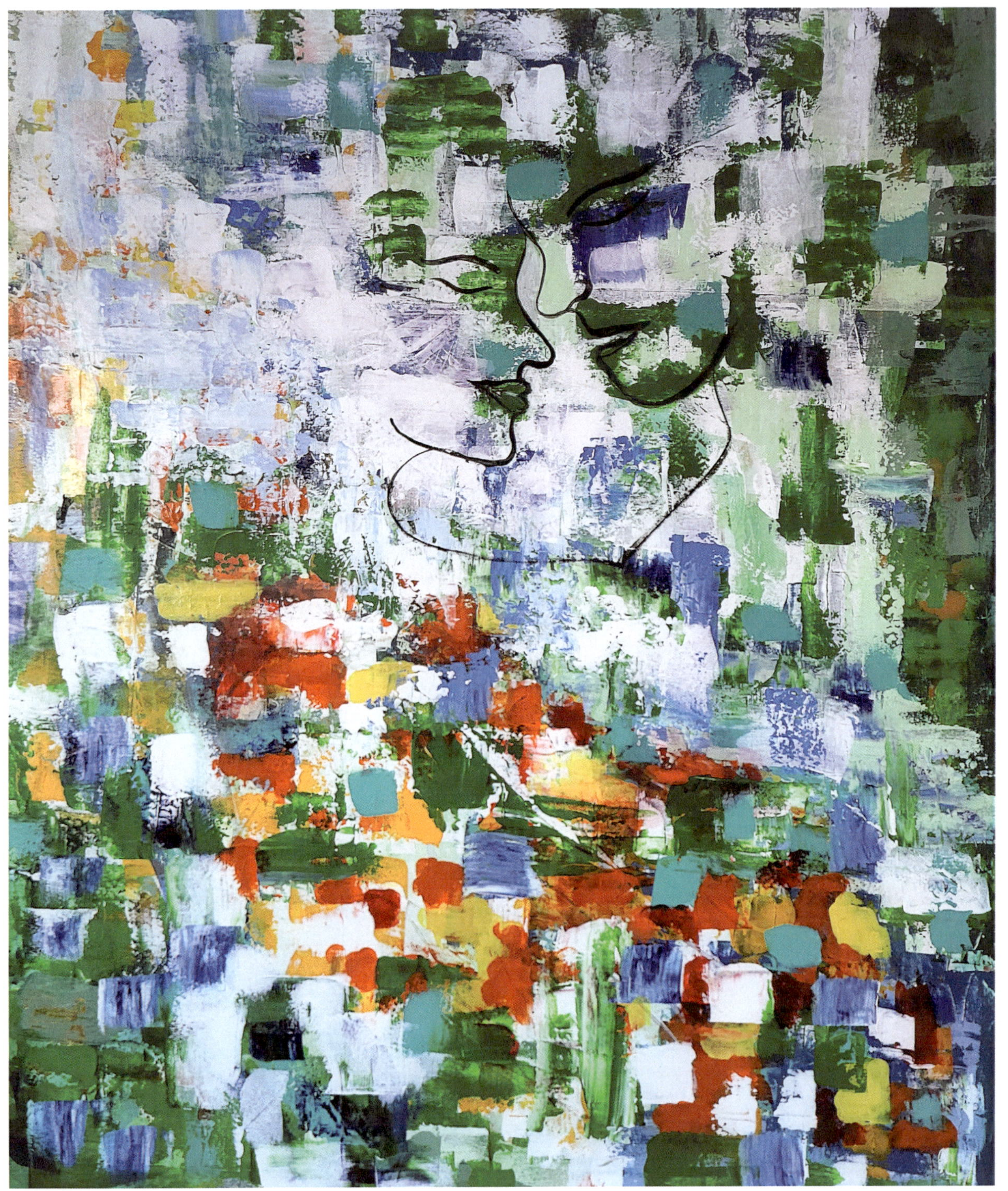

Love

Acrylic on canvas, 2023
5 x 4 feet

MY DAILY PRACTICE

Creating a heart-centred space

Every day, I set up a space where I ask for guidance.

I typically rise between 4 and 5:30 a.m. and spend an hour enjoying a cup of coffee. My meditation sessions average an hour, at minimum 20 minutes and maximum 90.

At about 5:50, I prepare to meditate, unroll my yoga mat and ensure comfort with my meditation bench and pillows. I light candles (fire) and sage (earth), and always ensure that I have a drink (water). I enjoy listening to sound (air) to help me focus on my heart. This is the sound of a "heartbeat in the womb."

After getting comfortable, I focus entirely on my heart and imagine that it is breathing. I imagine I am sitting inside my heart. When I am there, I focus on calmness and warmth. Within the latter space, I focus on present-tense statements of "I am …"

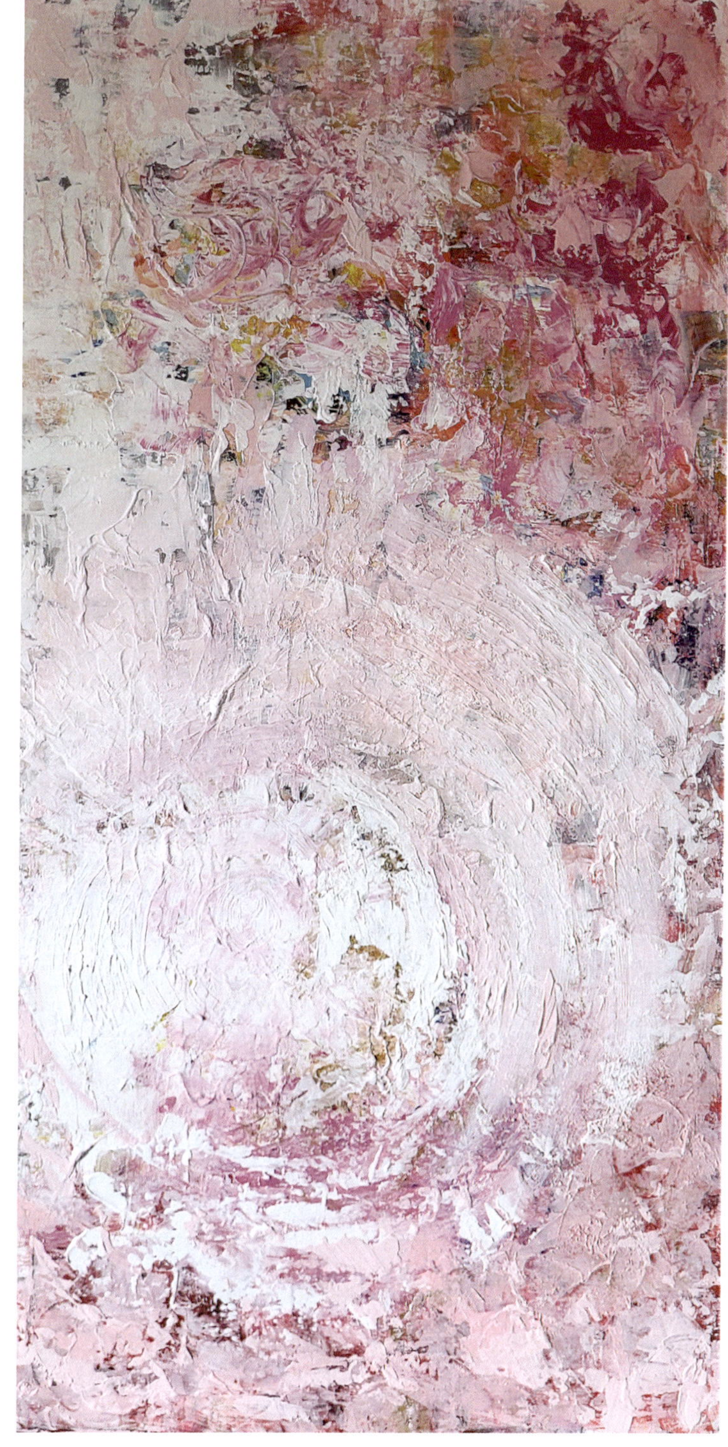

I AM WARM, SOFT, AND SILKY.

Meditation = Love

Acrylic on canvas, 2021
4 x 2 feet

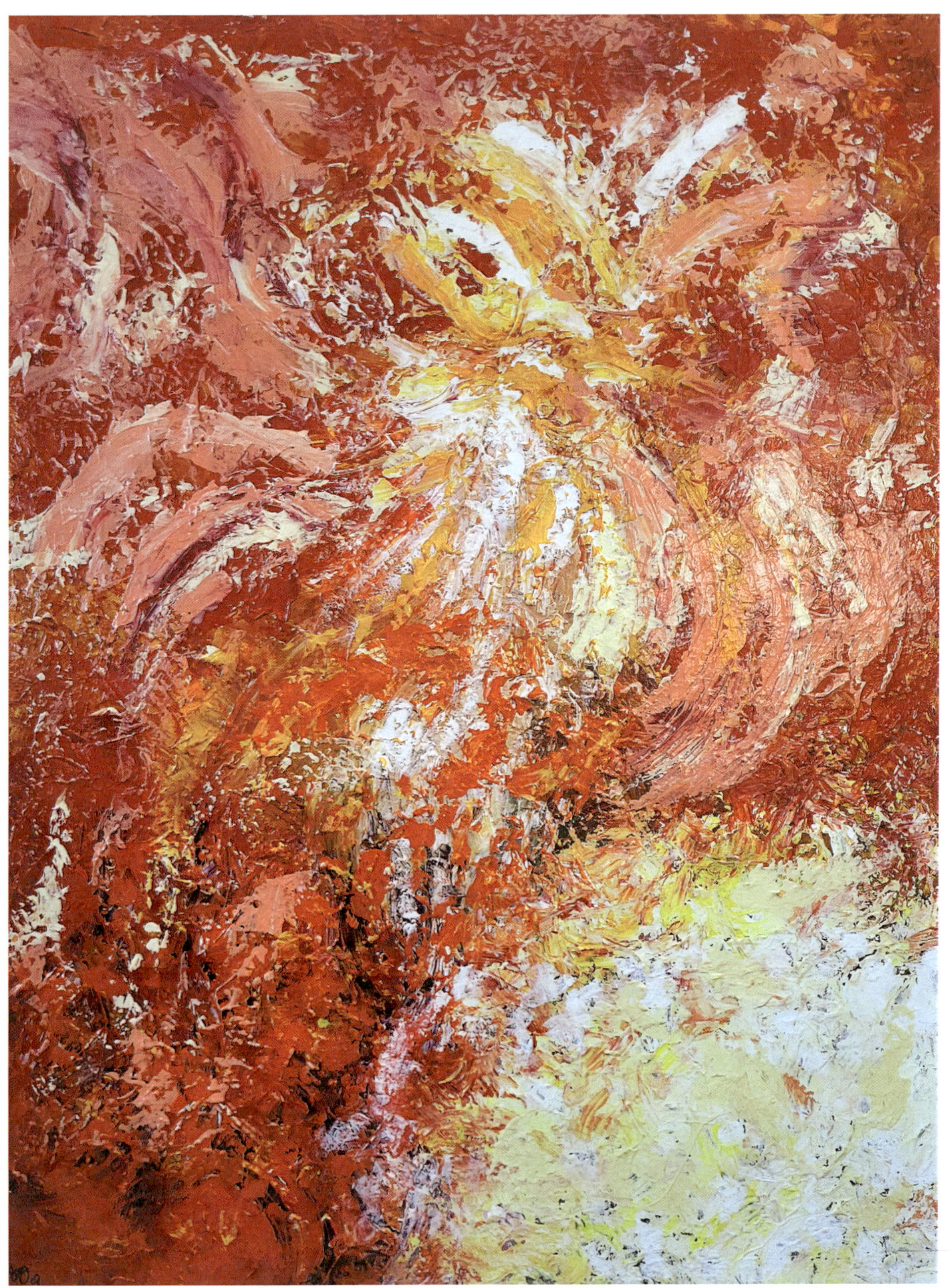

Activate me

Acrylic on canvas, 2021
4 x 3 feet

CONCLUSION

A heart-centred life

In March of 2020, I felt called to go deep into my soul to meditate. It took me a while to *listen* but when I finally did, the journey toward acknowledging my spiritual identity began.

Meditation and creative expression helped me discard a way of being that did not serve me. I now recognize that I could never feel whole until I acknowledged heart/Spirit in my life.

I am now living in a heart-centred space where I am connected to and communicating with my spiritual guides.

I admit that I do not know everything there is to know about them and the power that sits in my heart. What I do know is that they must be respected and approached with a willingness to learn and trust. I acknowledge I have much more to learn from Spirit.

Finally, we are living in unprecedented times. Mother Earth is letting us know we need to employ our personal medicine power and connect with our guides. And that we must rely on their help going forward.

Only when all is in alignment will we be able to move forward in a healthy way.

Respect, respect, respect!

Acrylic on canvas, 2023
3 x 4 feet

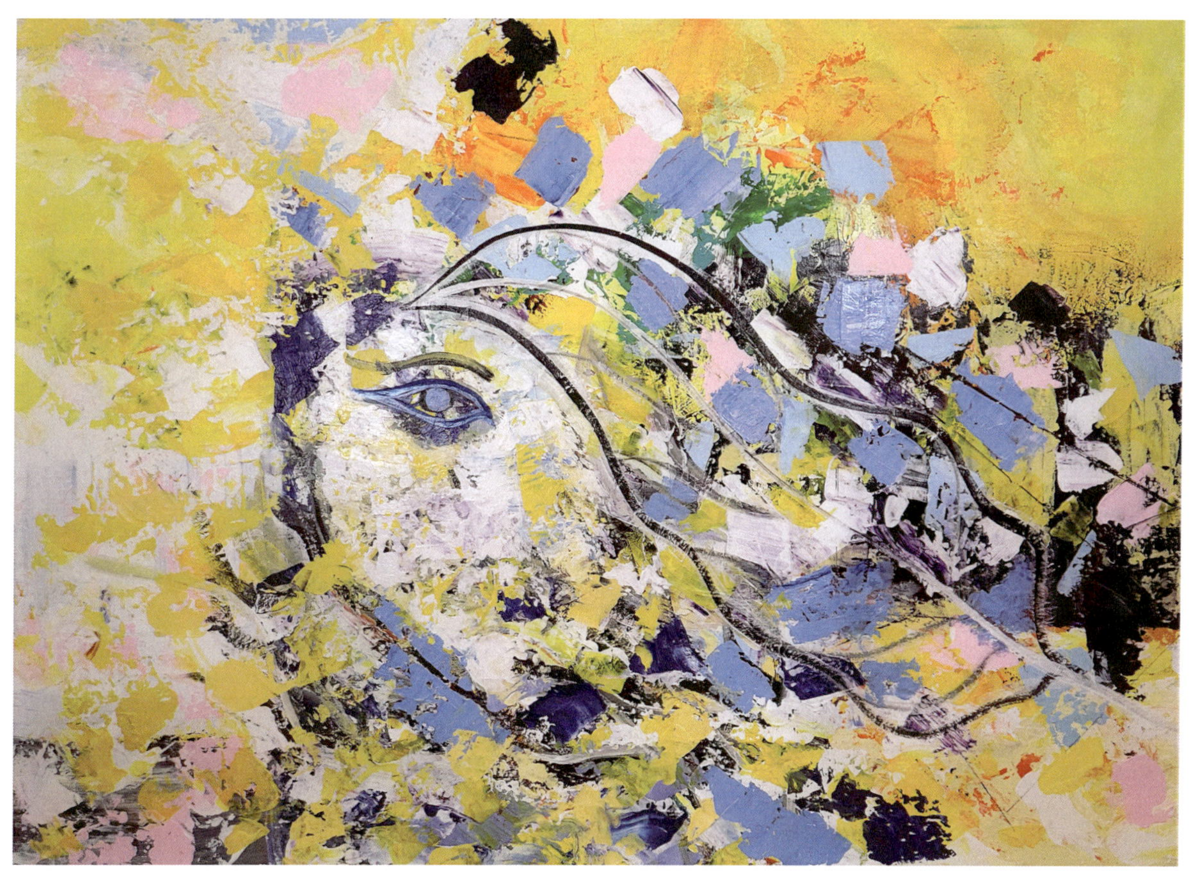

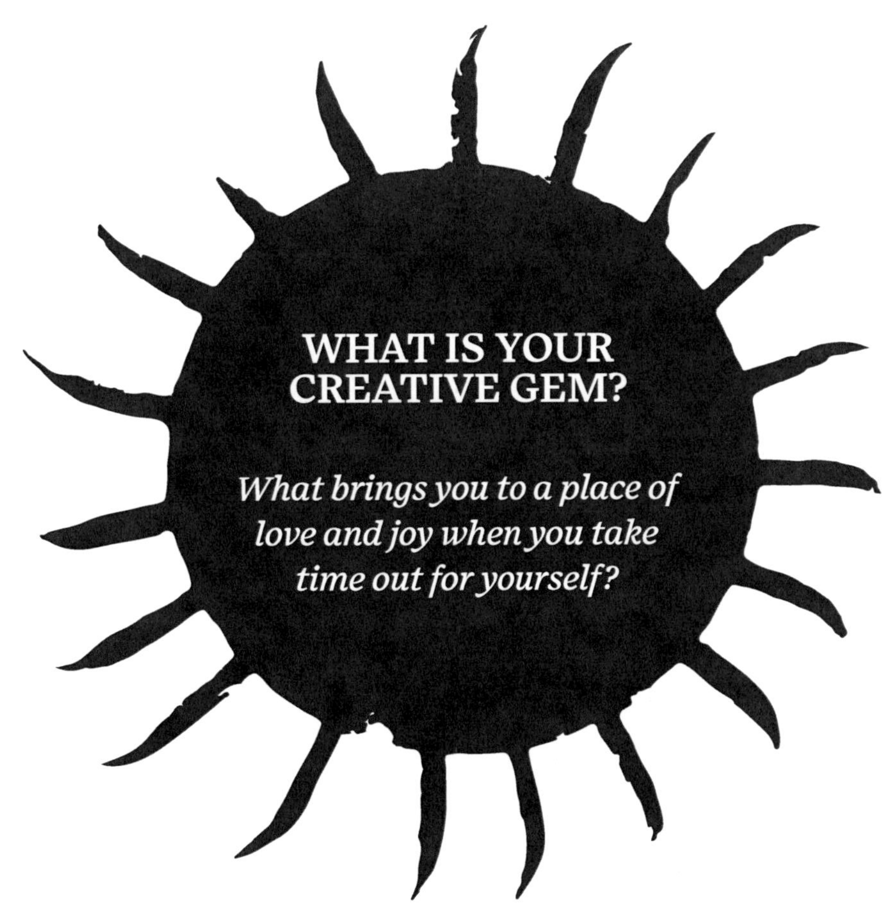
WHAT IS YOUR
CREATIVE GEM?

What brings you to a place of
love and joy when you take
time out for yourself?